Written Basic English
for
Dyslexic Students

Transition to the Classroom

MARIETTA LAING BIDDLE

Texas Scottish Rite Hospital for Children

Dallas, Texas

This book is dedicated to Dr. Lucius Waites
without whose assistance and encouragement
it would not have been completed.

Educators Publishing Service, Inc.

31 Smith Place, Cambridge, MA 02138-1089

May 2000 Printing   ISBN 0-8388-2322-X

Contents

Introduction

This book was developed because some of our students requested more help with English. It was evident from their homework assignments that they needed the most assistance with grammar and syntax.

Our past experience has shown that the following outline of the *Written Basic English* program is suitable for students who have completed remedial training and the oral English section of the *Dyslexia Training Program* tapes or have worked on the equivalent skills in the *Literacy Program*.

I. Parts of Speech
II. Syntax
III. Punctuation and Capitalization
IV. Practice Exercises
    Answer Key

The book's first three sections are a reference guide to the basic grammar and punctuation rules of standard English. The fourth section presents an opportunity for practice. Using the Answer Key booklet enables students to check their work on the Part A exercises.

The book may be used (1) to teach students the basic structure of written American English; or (2) as a review for students who have had training and want to study the reference section, work the practice exercises, and check their own work using the separate Answer Key.

Before beginning the *Written Basic English* program, students should prepare a companion notebook, divided into four sections. In the first section, students should write their answers to the book's Part B exercises. In the second section, they should list corrected spellings of misspelled words from their creative work. Students should write new vocabulary words in the third section. For the final section, which concerns knowledge development, students should research the book's literature, geography, history, science, art, and music references. This final section helps students to expand their background knowledge and build a foundation for written expression.

It is our hope that these efforts will help students become independent learners, and that through improving their speaking and writing skills, students will gain the self-confidence necessary to achieve their goals.

Parts of Speech

Parts of speech are the building blocks we use to construct sentences. The way a word is used in a sentence determines its part of speech.

> **EXAMPLE:**   The <u>rose</u> delighted her.
> rose—noun
> The smoke <u>rose</u> from the chimney.
> rose—verb

Knowing the parts of speech and their use in a sentence is essential if the writer wishes to express his or her thoughts clearly and correctly.

Basic facts and examples of the eight parts of speech are presented here and may be referred to whenever necessary.

NOUNS

A noun is the *name* of a person, place, thing, or idea.

Common noun is the name of a person, place, or thing.

> **EXAMPLES:**   boy, city, book

Proper noun is the name of a particular person, place, or thing. Proper nouns are capitalized.

> **EXAMPLES:**   Bill, Rome, *Treasure Island*

1. *Concrete nouns* name things one can see or touch.

   > **EXAMPLES:**   spoon, car, pancake, mountain

2. *Abstract nouns* name qualities and ideas.

   > **EXAMPLES:**   truth, goodness, courage, kindness

3. *Collective nouns* name a group of people, animals, or things that are thought of as a unit.

   > **EXAMPLES:**   team, committee, herd, flock

   If individuals act as a unit, the noun is singular.

   > **EXAMPLE:**   The committee is meeting at noon.

   If individuals act separately, the noun is plural.

   > **EXAMPLE:**   The committee were divided in their opinions.

Number

A noun can be either singular or plural.

Singular—one
Plural—more than one

Plurals can be formed by:

1. adding *s*

   EXAMPLE: room—rooms

2. adding *es* if the base word ends in a sibilant sound (for example, *s*, *sh*, *x*, *ch*, *z*)

   EXAMPLES: brush—brushes   tax—taxes

3. changing *y* to *i* and adding *es* if the *y* follows a consonant

   EXAMPLE: party—parties

4. adding *s* or *es* to words ending in *o*

   EXAMPLES: radio—radios   tomato—tomatoes

5. changing *f* or *fe* to *ves*

   EXAMPLES: self—selves   wife—wives

Gender

A noun can be masculine, feminine, common, or neuter.

Masculine	male	man
Feminine	female	woman
Common	either male or female	child
Neuter	neither male nor female	box

Person

Nouns do not change form to show person as pronouns do.

Nouns are usually in the third person, but nouns in direct address are in the second person.

EXAMPLE: How are you, Mrs. Silva?

Case

Case shows the use of a noun in a sentence.

Nominative

A noun is in the nominative case if it is

1. The subject

   EXAMPLE: The <u>author</u> wrote tirelessly.

2. A predicate nominative

   EXAMPLE: Charles Dickens is my favorite <u>author</u>.

3. In direct address

   EXAMPLE: <u>Mr. Dickens</u>, when did you tour the United States?

4. In apposition

   EXAMPLE: Charles Dickens, the <u>author</u> of *Bleak House*, lived in England.

Objective

A noun is in the objective case if it is

1. A direct object

   EXAMPLE: The pirates hid the <u>gold</u>.

2. An indirect object

   EXAMPLE: Juan sent <u>Fran</u> the package.

3. An object of the preposition

   EXAMPLE: The star twinkled in the <u>sky</u>.

4. In apposition with a word in the objective case

   EXAMPLE: Captain Nemo commanded the *Nautilus*, a <u>submarine</u>.

Possessive

A noun is in the possessive case if it shows ownership or possession. Nouns have singular and plural possessive forms.

EXAMPLES: man's jacket (singular possessive)
men's jackets (plural possessive)
girl's book (singular possessive)
girls' books (plural possessive)

To form possessives of a singular noun, add an apostrophe and an *s* (*'s*)

To form the possessive of a plural noun, add an apostrophe if the word ends in *s* (*s'*), or add an apostrophe and an *s* (*'s*) if the plural form does not end in *s*.

PRONOUNS

A pronoun takes the place of a noun.

The five kinds of pronouns are *personal, interrogative, demonstrative, indefinite,* and *relative.*

Personal pronouns refer to people and indicate by form whether a person is speaking, spoken to, or spoken about.

First person (person speaking)
I, my, mine, me, we, our, ours, us

EXAMPLE: <u>I</u> asked for the list.

Second person (person spoken to)
you, your, yours

EXAMPLE: <u>You</u> have three copies.

Third person (person or thing spoken about)
he, his, him, she, her, hers, it, its,
they, their, theirs, them

EXAMPLE: <u>She</u> listed the items alphabetically.

Compound personal pronouns are formed by adding *self* or *selves* to personal pronouns. Compound personal pronouns can be reflexive or intensive. A *reflexive* pronoun reflects or refers back to the subject.

EXAMPLES: I hurt <u>myself</u> last week.
The cook burned <u>herself</u>.

Intensive pronouns are used for emphasis.

EXAMPLES: I *myself* drove to the station.
The actors *themselves* performed the stunts.

Interrogative pronouns are words used to ask questions.

who, whom, whose, which, what

They may be used as the subject, object of the verb, or object of a preposition.

> **EXAMPLES:**   <u>Who</u> will bake the bread?
> The class read <u>what</u>?
> The cake was iced by <u>whom</u>?

Demonstrative pronouns point out definite people or things.

this, these, that, those

> **EXAMPLES:**   <u>This</u> is the museum.
> Do you like <u>these</u>?
> <u>That</u> isn't my choice.
> I purchased <u>those</u>.

Indefinite pronouns do not refer to definite people or things.

all, any, both, each, either, neither, few, many, none, some, several, anybody, everybody, nobody, somebody, no one, someone, everyone, one, anyone

> **EXAMPLES:**   Did <u>anyone</u> find a red wallet?
> <u>Both</u> of us attended the meeting.

Relative pronouns introduce subordinate clauses that describe or refer to another word in the sentence. The word to which a relative pronoun refers is called the antecedent.

who, which, that, what

If the antecedent is the name of a person, use *who*.

> **EXAMPLE:**   Bill knew the author <u>who</u> wrote the book.

If the antecedent is the name of a thing, and is followed by a nonrestrictive clause,* use *which*.

> **EXAMPLE:**   She climbed Mt. Everest, <u>which</u> is the highest mountain in the world.

If the antecedent is the name of a person or thing and is followed by a restrictive clause,* use *that*.

> **EXAMPLES:**   The artist <u>that</u> painted the dancers was Degas.
> The horse <u>that</u> won the race was Citation.

The word *what* does not have an antecedent. It refers to an idea and is not used when referring to persons or things.

> **EXAMPLE:**   He knew <u>what</u> was required.

6   * See p. 31 for information on restrictive and nonrestrictive clauses.

Number

Singular—one
Plural—more than one

Plurals of pronouns are formed differently than plurals of nouns. Pronouns change form.

EXAMPLES: I enjoyed the concert.
We enjoyed the concert.

Gender

Masculine	(male)	he
Feminine	(female)	she
Common	(either male or female)	they (the boys and the girls)
Neuter	(neither male nor female)	it

Person

First person	(person speaking)	I/we
Second person	(person spoken to)	you/you
Third person	(person spoken about)	he, she, it/they

Case

Case shows the use of a noun or pronoun in a sentence.

Nominative

A pronoun is in the nominative case if it is

1. The subject

   EXAMPLE: She must leave soon.

2. A predicate nominative

   EXAMPLE: It was they who made the request.

Objective

A pronoun is in the objective case if it is

1. A direct object

   EXAMPLE: The teller cashed it yesterday.

2. An indirect object

   EXAMPLE: Joe sent <u>her</u> roses.

3. An object of the preposition

   EXAMPLE: Henry will paint the house for <u>them</u>.

Possessive

A pronoun is in the possessive case if it shows possession or ownership.

Some indefinite pronouns form the possessive case with an apostrophe.

   EXAMPLE: <u>Somebody's</u> book was left on the table.

Personal pronouns already indicate possession, so an apostrophe is not necessary.

   EXAMPLES: <u>My</u> scarf is blue and green.
   Is <u>your</u> pencil on the desk?
   <u>Its</u> fur was matted.

VERBS

A verb is a word that shows action or state of being. A verb tells something about the subject of a sentence. Every sentence must have a verb.

A verb can show *action*:

1. "lively" physical action

   EXAMPLES: run, jump, sing

2. "quiet" action

   EXAMPLES: rest, stay

3. "mental" action

   EXAMPLES: remember, think, wish

A linking verb shows *state of being*. It connects or links a word in the predicate to the subject of the sentence.

These words may be used as linking verbs:

1. forms of the verb *to be*

   is, are, was, were, be, am, been

   EXAMPLE: Mr. Cook <u>is</u> a baker.

2. verbs of the senses

   see, hear, taste, smell, feel

   EXAMPLE: The coffee <u>smells</u> good.

Sometimes the words *look, seem, grow, appear, remain, sound,* and *stay* are used as linking verbs.

   EXAMPLE: The lake <u>seemed</u> calm.

An *auxiliary* verb is a helping verb. It helps the main verb in the sentence.

The main verb may be preceded by 1, 2, or 3 auxiliary verbs.

   EXAMPLES: Beth <u>is</u> knitting a sweater.
                   The laundry <u>should have been</u> finished by noon.

Examples of Auxiliary Verbs

can	may	shall	will
must	am	was	are
have	had	has	is
should	would	might	were
do	did	does	could

could be	shall be	will be
have been	had been	has been
should have	would have	must have
should have been	would have been	must have been

Class (or kind)

Transitive—verb has a receiver of the action

EXAMPLE: She sings a song.

Intransitive—verb does not have a receiver of the action

EXAMPLE: She sings in the choir.

Voice (if transitive)

Active—subject does the acting

EXAMPLE: We bought tickets for the play.

Passive—subject receives the action

EXAMPLE: The tickets were bought by us.

Only transitive verbs have voice.

An auxiliary verb must be used to express an idea in passive voice.

Tense (time)

Tense expresses when the action takes place.

Present—action now

EXAMPLE: I jump.

Past—action in the past

EXAMPLE: I jumped.

Future—action in the future

To form the future tense, use *shall* or *will* with the present tense.

EXAMPLES: I <u>shall</u> jump.
He <u>will</u> jump.

Present perfect—action completed or perfected now

To form the present perfect tense, use *have* or *has* with the past participle.

EXAMPLES: I <u>have</u> jumped.
She <u>has</u> jumped.

Past perfect—action completed or perfected in the past

To form the past perfect tense, use *had* with the past participle.

EXAMPLE: You <u>had</u> jumped.

Future perfect—action completed or perfected in the future. To form the future perfect tense, use *shall have* or *will have* with the past participle.

EXAMPLES: We <u>shall have</u> jumped.
They <u>will have</u> jumped.

Person

First person—person speaking

EXAMPLE: I rang the bell.

Second person—person spoken to

EXAMPLE: You rang the bell.

Third person—person spoken about

EXAMPLE: They rang the bell.

Number

Singular—one
Plural—more than one

A subject and verb must agree in number. A singular subject takes a singular verb. In the present tense, most singular verbs end with one *s*.

EXAMPLE: She sings.

A plural subject takes a plural verb. Most verbs that do **not** end with a single *s* are plural.

EXAMPLE: They sing.

Mood

Mood describes the way in which a statement is expressed.

Subjunctive is used to express a wish or a condition contrary to fact.

EXAMPLES: I wish I were nicer.
If I were you, I would read the book.

Indicative is used to state a fact or ask a question.

EXAMPLES: I am a student.
Have you finished the last project?

Imperative is used to express a command.

EXAMPLE: Check the schedule and pack the boxes.

Principal parts

Most verbs have three basic forms: present, past, and past participle.

Regular verb

Many verbs form the past tense and past participle by adding *-ed* to the present tense.

PRESENT	PAST	PAST PARTICIPLE
show	showed	showed
hope	hoped	hoped

Irregular verb

Some irregular verbs form the past tense and past participle by changing a vowel or changing the form of the verb. Sometimes the form remains the same for all the parts.

PRESENT	PAST	PAST PARTICIPLE
ring	rang	rung
do	did	done
cut	cut	cut

The present participle is formed by adding *-ing* to the present tense.

The perfect tenses are formed by adding the helping words *have, has, had,* or *shall/will have* to the past participle.

The principal parts of some irregular verbs are listed here. Use the dictionary to find the principal parts of other verbs.

PRESENT	PAST	PAST PARTICIPLE
see	saw	seen
go	went	gone
begin	began	begun
write	wrote	written

PRESENT	PAST	PAST PARTICIPLE
blow	blew	blown
swim	swam	swum
burst	burst	burst

Conjugation

A list of a verb's forms is called conjugation.

Regular verb—walk

PRESENT	PAST	PAST PARTICIPLE
walk	walked	walked

PRESENT TENSE

	SINGULAR	**PLURAL**
1st person	I walk	we walk
2nd person	you walk	you walk
3rd person	he, she, it walks	they walk

PAST TENSE

1st person	I walked	we walked
2nd person	you walked	you walked
3rd person	he, she, it walked	they walked

FUTURE TENSE

1st person	I shall walk	we shall walk
2nd person	you will walk	you will walk
3rd person	he, she, it will walk	they will walk

PRESENT PERFECT TENSE

1st person	I have walked	we have walked
2nd person	you have walked	you have walked
3rd person	he, she, it has walked	they have walked

PAST PERFECT TENSE

1st person	I had walked	we had walked
2nd person	you had walked	you had walked
3rd person	he, she, it had walked	they had walked

FUTURE PERFECT TENSE

	SINGULAR	**PLURAL**
1st person	I shall have walked	we shall have walked
2nd person	you will have walked	you will have walked
3rd person	he, she, it will have walked	they will have walked

Irregular verb—sing

PRESENT	PAST	PAST PARTICIPLE
sing	sang	sung

PRESENT TENSE

	SINGULAR	**PLURAL**
1st person	I sing	we sing
2nd person	you sing	you sing
3rd person	he, she, it sings	they sing

PAST TENSE

	SINGULAR	PLURAL
1st person	I sang	we sang
2nd person	you sang	you sang
3rd person	he, she, it sang	they sang

FUTURE TENSE

	SINGULAR	PLURAL
1st person	I shall sing	we shall sing
2nd person	you will sing	you will sing
3rd person	he, she, it will sing	they will sing

PRESENT PERFECT TENSE

	SINGULAR	PLURAL
1st person	I have sung	we have sung
2nd person	you have sung	you have sung
3rd person	he, she, it has sung	they have sung

PAST PERFECT TENSE

	SINGULAR	PLURAL
1st person	I had sung	we had sung
2nd person	you had sung	you had sung
3rd person	he, she, it had sung	they had sung

FUTURE PERFECT TENSE

	SINGULAR	PLURAL
1st person	I shall have sung	we shall have sung
2nd person	you will have sung	you will have sung
3rd person	he, she, it will have sung	they will have sung

To be

The verb *to be* is the most irregular. It may be used as an independent verb or an auxiliary verb.

PRESENT	PAST	PAST PARTICIPLE
be (am)	was	been

PRESENT TENSE

	SINGULAR	**PLURAL**
1st person	I am	we are
2nd person	you are	you are
3rd person	he, she, it is	they are

PAST TENSE

1st person	I was	we were
2nd person	you were	you were
3rd person	he, she, it was	they were

FUTURE TENSE

1st person	I shall be	we shall be
2nd person	you will be	you will be
3rd person	he, she, it will be	they will be

PRESENT PERFECT TENSE

1st person	I have been	we have been
2nd person	you have been	you have been
3rd person	he, she, it has been	they have been

PAST PERFECT TENSE

1st person	I had been	we had been
2nd person	you had been	you had been
3rd person	he, she, it had been	they had been

FUTURE PERFECT TENSE

1st person	I shall have been	we shall have been
2nd person	you will have been	you will have been
3rd person	he, she, it will have been	they will have been

Troublesome verbs

Confusion often arises when one must decide whether to use *lie* or *lay*, *sit* or *set*, and *rise* or *raise*.

Lie—to recline

This is an intransitive verb, and it never takes an object.

PRESENT	PAST	PAST PARTICIPLE
lie	lay	lain

EXAMPLE: The boys <u>lie</u> on their sleeping bags.

Lay—to put something down, to place

This is a transitive verb, and it takes a direct object.

PRESENT	PAST	PAST PARTICIPLE
lay	laid	laid

EXAMPLE: The hen <u>lays</u> an egg.

Sit—to rest

This is an intransitive verb, and it never takes an object.

PRESENT	PAST	PAST PARTICIPLE
sit	sat	sat

EXAMPLE: She <u>sits</u> at her desk.

Set—to place

This is a transitive verb, and it takes a direct object.

PRESENT	PAST	PAST PARTICIPLE
set	set	set

EXAMPLE: She <u>sets</u> the book on her desk.

Rise—to get up

This is an intransitive verb, and it never takes an object.

PRESENT	PAST	PAST PARTICIPLE
rise	rose	risen

EXAMPLE: The smoke <u>rises</u> in the air.

Raise—to lift

This is a transitive verb, and it takes a direct object.

PRESENT	PAST	PAST PARTICIPLE
raise	raised	raised

EXAMPLE: The students <u>raise</u> their hands.

Verbals—Participles, Gerunds, Infinitives

Participles, gerunds, and infinitives are derived from verbs and are used as other parts of speech.

Participle

A participle is a verb form that functions as an adjective and modifies some word in the sentence. A participle that ends in *-ing* is called a present participle. A participle that ends in *-ed* is called a past participle.

A participial phrase must be near the word it modifies.

Incorrect: Joan fell and skinned her knee, getting off the bus.
Correct: Getting off the bus, Joan fell and skinned her knee.

Gerund

A gerund is a verb form ending in *-ing* and used as a noun.

EXAMPLE: <u>Dancing</u> is an art.

Infinitive

An infinitive is a verb form used as a noun, an adjective, or an adverb. It is usually preceded by the word *to*.

When used as a noun, the infinitive may be the subject, direct object, or a predicate nominative.

EXAMPLES: <u>To win</u> was his aim. (subject)
Ellen likes <u>to read</u>. (direct object)
Our plan was <u>to rise</u> early. (predicate nominative)

When used as an adjective, it modifies a noun.

EXAMPLE: Alan has a car <u>to race</u>.

When used as an adverb, it modifies a verb, an adjective, or an adverb.

EXAMPLES: The major waited <u>to meet</u> the general.
The cookie dough is hard <u>to roll</u>.
That rope was strong enough <u>to hold</u> the boat.

Separating the two parts of an infinitive verb creates a split infinitive. Try to avoid these.

Correct: I want to read the book carefully.
Split infinitive: I want to carefully read the book.

ADJECTIVES

An adjective modifies a noun or a pronoun. It describes, limits, or points out information about a noun or pronoun.

Adjectives answer questions.

What kind?

A descriptive adjective describes or tells what kind. It tells color, size, shape, or type.

EXAMPLES: <u>red</u> top, <u>wider</u> road, <u>square</u> box, <u>old</u> hat

How many?

An adjective that limits tells how many—the number or quantity.

EXAMPLES: <u>three</u> plums, <u>several</u> books

Which one?

An adjective that points out tells which one.

EXAMPLES: <u>this</u> pencil, <u>these</u> crayons, <u>that</u> coat, <u>those</u> belts

There are three degrees of comparison for an adjective:

1. Positive   <u>simple</u> quality

   EXAMPLE: great

2. Comparative   <u>more</u> quality

   EXAMPLE: greater

3. Superlative   <u>most</u> quality

   EXAMPLE: greatest

There are three ways to change an adjective's degree of comparison:

1. Add -er and -est to the positive degree of one-syllable words to form the comparative and superlative degrees.

2. Add more and most to the positive degree of words of more than one-syllable to form the comparative and superlative degrees.

3. Change the form of some adjectives to form the comparative and superlative degrees.

EXAMPLES:

Positive	small	beautiful	good
Comparative	smaller	more beautiful	better
Superlative	smallest	most beautiful	best

An adjective usually comes before the noun it modifies.

EXAMPLES: <u>soft</u> cloth, <u>nine</u> cows

When adjectives are subject complements, they follow a linking verb. These are also called predicate adjectives.

EXAMPLES: The car is <u>blue</u>.
An apple tastes <u>good</u>.

ADVERBS

An adverb describes or modifies a verb, an adjective, or another adverb.

EXAMPLES: She screamed <u>loudly</u>.
The <u>exceedingly</u> good player scored ninety points.
He spoke <u>very</u> boastfully about himself.

Adverbs answer questions:

Where?	(place)	there, here
When?	(time)	soon, lately
How?	(manner)	loudly, fast
To what extent?	(frequency)	twice

Not is an adverb. It is used as an interrupter.

                                adv.
EXAMPLE: He <u>did</u> not <u>hear</u> the doorbell.

Adverbs usually come after the verb, and they often end in -ly.
An adjective + ly = an adverb.

EXAMPLE: clear + ly = clearly

Adjectives or Adverbs

Be careful with the words *good, well, real,* and *really.* They are often misused. If you are trying to decide which word to use, ask yourself, "What does this word do in the sentence?"

Good is an adjective that means favorable, satisfactory.

> **Correct:** This juice tastes <u>good</u>.
> **Incorrect:** He reads <u>good</u>.

The adverb *well* means in a pleasing or proper manner, skillfully.

> **EXAMPLE:** He reads <u>well</u>.

When used as an adjective, *well* means in good condition, healthy.

> **EXAMPLE:** Anna felt <u>well</u>.

Real is an adjective that means genuine, not imaginary, not artificial.

> **EXAMPLE:** In the new version of the movie, they used <u>real</u> dalmations.

Really is an adverb that means actually or without question.

> **Correct:** Mother was <u>really</u> pleased with the twins' progress.
> **Incorrect:** Mother was <u>real</u> pleased with the twins' progress.

PREPOSITIONS

Prepositions show the relationship of nouns or pronouns to other words in the sentence. The noun or pronoun that follows a preposition is called the object of the preposition. The preposition and its object are called a prepositional phrase.

A preposition **must** have an object to complete its meaning.

> **prep.   obj. of prep.**
> **EXAMPLE:** Smoke goes <u>up</u> the <u>chimney</u>.
> *Up* by itself is an adverb.
> As a preposition, *up* needs an object to complete the meaning.

Adjective prepositional phrases modify nouns or pronouns.

Adverbial prepositional phrases modify verbs, adjectives, or adverbs.

LIST OF PREPOSITIONS

about	behind	for	over
above	below	from	since
across	beneath	in	through
after	beside	inside	to
against	between	into	toward
along	beyond	like	under
among	by	near	until
around	down	of	up
at	during	off	upon
before	except	on	with

CONJUNCTIONS

Conjunctions join or connect words or groups of words. There are three kinds of conjunctions.

1. *Coordinate Conjunctions* join words or clauses of equal value.

   EXAMPLES: and, but, or, nor, for
   John played the violin, <u>and</u> Andy played the piano.

2. *Subordinate Conjunctions* join clauses of unequal value.

   EXAMPLES: if, since, unless, as, because
   We will read a story <u>if</u> we have time.

3. *Correlative Conjunctions* are used in pairs.

   EXAMPLES: neither—nor, either—or, both—and
   <u>Neither</u> Jenny <u>nor</u> Maria attended the picnic.

INTERJECTIONS

Interjections are words that show strong feeling. They are followed by an exclamation point. Interjections are not related grammatically to other words in the sentence.

Common Interjections

Ah!	Hey!
Aha!	Hurrah!
Ahoy!	Oh!
Alas!	Ouch!
Bah!	Shoo!
Bravo!	Ugh!
Enough!	Well!
Good!	Whew!
Ha!	Whoa!

Syntax

Syntax is the structure of a language; it is the way in which words are put together to form sentences.

A *sentence* is a group of words that has a subject and a predicate. A sentence expresses a complete thought.

A *subject* is a word or group of words about which something is said. The complete subject is the simple subject (noun or pronoun) and its modifiers.

A *predicate* is a word or group of words that makes a statement about the subject. The complete predicate is the verb and its modifiers and complements.

A *diagram* is a plan or drawing that makes something easier to understand. A sentence diagram explains the structure of a sentence; it is a visual plan or blueprint of the sentence.

Basic facts and examples of sentences are presented here and may be referred to whenever necessary.

Sentence

A *sentence* is a group of words that expresses a complete thought.

Each sentence must have a *subject* and a *predicate*.

The subject and predicate must agree in number.

EXAMPLE: Singular subject   Singular verb   Plural subject   Plural verb

Bell | rings   Bells | ring

Sentences begin with capital letters. The thought expressed by the sentence determines the end punctuation.

There are four kinds of sentences:

1. A *declarative* sentence makes a statement. It is punctuated with a period.

   EXAMPLE: Jane read the book.
   (Regular word order, subject is first)

2. An *interrogative* sentence asks a question. It is punctuated with a question mark.

   EXAMPLE: Have you saved ten dollars?
   (Inverted word order, verb before subject)

3. An *imperative* sentence commands or orders. It is punctuated with a period.

   EXAMPLE: Copy the list.
   (The subject *you* is understood.)

4. An *exclamatory* sentence shows strong feeling. It is punctuated with an exclamation point.

   EXAMPLE: Help! The spark from the fireplace is igniting the rug!

A *phrase* is a part of a sentence. It has no subject or predicate. It is a group of related words that describes the subject or predicate.

A prepositional phrase may be adjectival or adverbial depending upon the part of speech of the word it modifies.

EXAMPLES: The trunk in the attic contained the costumes.
(adjectival prepositional phrase)

```
trunk    |   contained   |  costumes
_____
The      |               |    the
in  |  attic
        |___
           the
```

Joe put the roast in the oven.
(adverbial prepositional phrase)

```
Joe |  put              |  roast
        in  |  oven          the
               the
```

A *clause* is a group of words that contains a subject and predicate.

There are independent clauses and dependent clauses.

1. An *independent clause* stands alone. It is an important clause, and it expresses a complete idea.

   EXAMPLE: I ride on the bus.

2. A *dependent clause* depends on the rest of the sentence. It is introduced by a word that connects it to an independent clause. Since a dependent clause is of lesser value, it needs the independent clause to complete the meaning of the sentence.

EXAMPLE: When I ride on the bus (dependent clause),
I am late for school (independent clause).

A sentence *fragment* is an incomplete statement.

EXAMPLE: Before I arrived.

Sentences may be simple, compound, or complex.

1. A *simple sentence* contains a subject and a predicate.

   EXAMPLE: Dana | sang

2. A *compound sentence* contains two independent clauses joined by a coordinate conjunction (*and, but, or, nor, for*).

   EXAMPLE: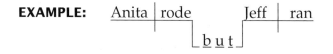

3. A *complex sentence* contains one independent clause and one dependent clause joined by a subordinate conjunction (*if, since, unless, because, although*).

   EXAMPLE: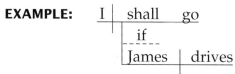

NOTE: The word *there* is sometimes used to introduce a sentence, but it is never the subject of a sentence. When it is used as an introductory word, it is an *expletive*.

An expletive is an extra word added to fill up space.

An expletive, like a noun in direct address, is independent of the sentence parts, and in a sentence diagram it is set on a line above the sentence.

EXAMPLE: Expletive

There are three apples in the sack.

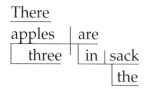

EXAMPLE: Direct address

Sue, answer the phone.

```
Sue
(you) | answer | phone
                    | the
```

Complements are words that complete the thought of a sentence. Direct objects, indirect objects, predicate nominatives, and predicate adjectives are complements.

1. A *direct object* receives the action of the verb. To find the direct object name the action verb and ask *what* or *whom*.

    EXAMPLE: The boy caught the fish.

    ```
    boy | caught | fish
    The           | the
    ```

2. An *indirect object* tells *to whom/what* or *for whom/what* the action of the verb is done.

    EXAMPLE: She gave him the cake.

    ```
    She | gave | cake
         X | him | the
    ```

    NOTE: The indirect object usually comes before the direct object in a sentence. The indirect object tells to whom or for whom something was done, but the words *to* or *for* are **not** always expressed in the sentence. X represents the words *to* or *for* in the sentence diagram.

3. A *predicate nominative* is a noun in the predicate that completes the sentence. It follows a linking verb and refers back to the subject.

    EXAMPLE: Mrs. Smith is a teacher.

    ```
    Mrs. Smith | is \ teacher
                       | a
    ```

4. A *predicate adjective* is an adjective in the predicate that completes the sentence. It follows a linking verb and describes the subject.

EXAMPLE: The sun is hot.

sun | is \ hot
⌐The

Punctuation and Capitalization

The word punctuation comes from the Latin word *punctus* (point). "Pointing manuscripts" began as a visual aid to help people read aloud in church and at social gatherings.

Punctuation marks make the meaning of a sentence clear and help the reader understand what the writer is saying.

Basic facts and examples of punctuation and capitalization are presented here and may be referred to whenever necessary.

COMMAS

Commas indicate a pause, set off words and groups of words, and make the meaning of a sentence clear. Commas are needed in the following situations:

1. *Direct address* When a person's name is called, the name is a noun in direct address. A noun in direct address is never the subject of a sentence.

   EXAMPLE: <u>Marsha</u>, did you leave your umbrella at the library?

2. *Appositive* A group of words used to explain a noun or pronoun is called an appositive.

   EXAMPLE: Eugene Field, <u>a famous poet</u>, wrote verses for children.

3. *Series* A list of at least three related words is called a series. Use commas between words and before the conjunction that precedes the last word of the series. If the final comma is omitted, the meaning of the sentence is sometimes changed.

   EXAMPLES: We will tour Sweden, Germany, France, and Italy.
   Kate, Bill, and Bob were elected to the student council.

   NOTE: If the final comma is omitted in the second sentence, the sentence then appears as follows:

   Kate, Bill and Bob were elected to the student council.

   A reader may assume that Kate is a noun in direct address and only Bill and Bob were elected to the council.

4. *Independent elements* *Yes* and *no* are examples of independent elements.

   EXAMPLE: Yes, I will attend the first session.

5. Before a *coordinate conjunction*   A comma is placed before a coordinate conjunction that joins two independent clauses.

EXAMPLE: *I Know Why the Caged Bird Sings* was written by Maya Angelou, and *A Room of One's Own* was written by Virginia Woolf.

6. After a *dependent clause*   A comma is placed after a dependent clause that begins a sentence.

EXAMPLE: If she has difficulty solving crossword puzzles, she should purchase a crossword puzzle dictionary.

7. *Nonrestrictive clause*   A nonrestrictive clause is not necessary for the meaning of the sentence. It merely supplies additional information. It is set off by commas.

EXAMPLE: That woman, who is wearing the red jacket, is the speaker.

8. *Restrictive clause*   A restrictive clause is necessary for the meaning of the sentence. It supplies important information and is not set off by commas.

EXAMPLE: The woman who returned your book should be rewarded.

9. *Parenthetical expressions*   These are set off by commas when they are used as interrupters. *I think, on the other hand, by the way,* and *of course* are parenthetical expressions.

EXAMPLE: Our budget, of course, will determine the length of our vacation.

10. *Direct quotations*   A comma is used to set off direct quotations.

EXAMPLE: "I read the book before the meeting," explained Mrs. Graves.

11. *Dates and Addresses*   Commas separate each item in dates and addresses unless they are at the end of a sentence.

EXAMPLES: The team met on October 9, 1994, on the west side of the stadium.

She ordered the film from the studio at 125 Belton Drive, Sherman, IL 61223.

12. *Salutations and Closings* Commas are used after the salutation in a friendly letter and after the closing in any letter.

    EXAMPLES: Dear Sally,
                         Sincerely yours,

SEMICOLONS

A semicolon shows a longer pause than a comma and a shorter pause than a colon.

A semicolon is used between the independent clauses of a compound sentence if there is no coordinate conjunction.

    EXAMPLE: He missed the bus; his father had to drive him to school.

A semicolon is used to separate the words in a series if commas are used within each part of the series.

    EXAMPLE: She bought balloons, whistles, and books; made a cake, cookies, and candy; selected flowers, music, and invitations for the party.

COLONS

A colon shows the strongest break. It introduces a list, a description, or an explanation.

    EXAMPLE: The picnic basket contained many items: sandwiches, fruit, cookies, lemonade, a tablecloth, plates, and cups.

A colon is used after the salutation in a business letter.

    EXAMPLE: Dear Sir:

A colon is placed between the hour and minutes when writing the time.

    EXAMPLE: 5:07

APOSTROPHES

An apostrophe is used to show possession or ownership.

    EXAMPLE: Mary's bracelet was in the box.

An apostrophe is also used to show a contraction.

    EXAMPLE: It's too late to order the cards.

QUOTATION MARKS

A person's exact words are enclosed in quotation marks. If a period or comma follows a direct quotation, it is placed inside the quotation marks. If the quotation is a question or exclamation, the appropriate mark goes inside the quotation marks.

EXAMPLE: "Members of the ski club will meet on Friday," announced Carlos.

If a quotation appears within a quotation, single quotation marks are used.

EXAMPLE: "Can you identify the author of the statement 'to thine own self be true'?" asked Ms. Mendez.

ABBREVIATIONS

Abbreviations and initials are followed by a period.

A few common abbreviations are listed here. Others may be found in the dictionary.

Mr.	a title for a man	P.M.	post meridiem (after noon)
Ms.	a title for a woman	A.D.	anno Domini (in the year of our Lord)
Mrs.	a title for a woman that indicates that she is married	B.C.	before Christ
Dr.	a title for a doctor	e.g.	exempli gratia (for example)
A.M.	ante meridiem (before noon)	i.e.	id est (that is)

CAPITALIZATION

Capital letters are used in certain situations according to standard usage. Some of the situations are listed below.

1. First word of a sentence and each line of poetry

EXAMPLE: Once upon a midnight dreary, while I pondered,
      weak and weary,
Over many a quaint and curious volume of
      forgotten lore—
While I nodded, nearly napping, suddenly there
      came a tapping,
As of someone gently rapping, rapping at my
      chamber door.

From *The Raven*, by Edgar Allan Poe

2. Proper nouns and adjectives derived from proper nouns

    EXAMPLES: Mark, French toast

3. Person's title

    EXAMPLES: Dr. Lopez, Senator Martin

4. Geographical names

    EXAMPLES: Yosemite Falls, Florida Keys

5. Days of the week, months of the year, and holidays

    EXAMPLES: Friday, September, Thanksgiving

6. Deity

    EXAMPLES: God, Bible, Koran

7. Titles of books

    EXAMPLES: *Treasure Island, Aesop's Fables*

8. Regions of the country

    EXAMPLES: the Southwest, the Northeast

    NOTE: North, south, east, and west are *not* capitalized when they show direction.

    EXAMPLE: His house is north of the park.

School subjects are *not* capitalized unless they are language classes.

    EXAMPLES: algebra, Spanish, English

Seasons of the year are not capitalized.

    EXAMPLES: fall, winter, spring, summer

Practice Exercises

NOUNS

Statement

A *noun* is the name of a person, place, thing, or idea.

A. Directions

Label these nouns. Write *person, place, thing*, or *idea* on the blanks beside the words.

1. teacher   _____

2. spoon   _____

3. ruffle   _____

4. movie theater   _____

5. actor   _____

6. post office   _____

7. nail   _____

8. happiness   _____

9. plumber   _____

10. boat   _____

11. valor   _____

12. hospital   _____

B. Directions

Make a list of twelve nouns. Include three people, three places, four things, and two ideas.

NOUNS

Statement

A *noun* is the name of a person, place, thing, or idea.

A *proper noun* is the name of a *particular* person, place, or thing.

A. Directions

Decide if the noun is *common* or *proper*, and write an X in the correct column.

	COMMON	PROPER
1. desk	_____	_____
2. tuesday	_____	_____
3. october	_____	_____
4. farmer	_____	_____
5. ivanhoe	_____	_____
6. muffin	_____	_____
7. mark twain	_____	_____
8. fork	_____	_____
9. excalibur	_____	_____
10. riddle	_____	_____

B. Directions

Write a sentence using a common noun. Label the common noun *c*.

Write a sentence using a proper noun. Label the proper noun *p*.

EXAMPLES: The tourist walked down the <u>street</u>.
c above street

Unter den Linden is a famous street in Berlin.
p above Unter den Linden

NOUNS

Statement

A *noun* is the name of a person, place, thing, or idea.

A *proper noun* is the name of a *particular* person, place, or thing.

A. Directions

In the second column, write a *proper noun* that corresponds with each common noun in the first column. Remember to capitalize proper nouns.

COMMON NOUNS	PROPER NOUNS
1. lake	_____
2. book	_____
3. state	_____
4. street	_____
5. queen	_____
6. author	_____
7. city	_____
8. ocean	_____
9. mountains	_____
10. continent	_____

B. Directions

Write two sentences; use a common noun and a proper noun in *each* sentence.

Label the common nouns *c*.

Label the proper nouns *p*.

EXAMPLES:
               c   c   p

The lake on the California-Nevada boundary is named Tahoe.

                 p   c   p

The Taj Mahal is a tomb located in India.

NOUNS

Statement

A *noun* is the name of a person, place, thing, or idea.

A *proper noun* is the name of *particular* person, place, or thing.

A. Directions

Label these nouns. Write *person*, *place*, or *thing* on the blanks beside the nouns. Then write *c* for *common* and *p* for *proper*.

1. doctor _____

2. rio grande valley _____

3. button _____

4. pipe _____

5. sister _____

6. box _____

7. central park _____

8. judge _____

9. zoo _____

10. jonathan swift _____

B. Directions

List a common noun and proper noun that name a person, a common noun and proper noun that name a place, and a common noun and proper noun that name a thing.

EXAMPLES: president   George Washington
city   Rome
violin   Stradivarius

NOUNS

Statement

A *noun* is the name of a person, place, thing, or idea.

A *proper noun* is the name of a *particular* person, place, or thing.

A. Directions

Write a *common noun* to identify each proper noun, and label it *person, place,* or *thing*.

PROPER NOUNS	COMMON NOUNS	PERSON, PLACE, THING
1. *Mona Lisa*	_____	_____
2. "The Ant and the Grasshopper"	_____	_____
3. Leonardo da Vinci	_____	_____
4. Johannes Brahms	_____	_____
5. Nile	_____	_____
6. Sahara	_____	_____
7. Robert E. Lee	_____	_____
8. Yellowstone	_____	_____
9. Chicago	_____	_____
10. "The Legend of Sleepy Hollow"	_____	_____

B. Directions

List another proper noun for each of the common nouns above.

NOUNS

Statement

A *concrete* noun names things one can see or touch.

An *abstract* noun names qualities or ideas.

A *collective* noun names a group of people, animals, or things that are thought of as a unit.

A. Directions

Classify these nouns. Write *concrete, abstract,* or *collective* on the blanks beside the words.

1. jar   _____

2. strength   _____

3. committee   _____

4. herd   _____

5. book   _____

6. affection   _____

7. truth   _____

8. group   _____

9. contentment   _____

10. crate   _____

B. Directions

List two *concrete* nouns, two *abstract* nouns, and two *collective* nouns.

EXAMPLES: lamp   love   troop
                    chest   power   flock

NOUNS

Statement

A *concrete* noun names things one can see or touch.

An *abstract* noun names qualities or ideas.

A *collective* noun names a group of people, animals, or things that are thought of as a unit.

A. Directions

Classify these nouns. Write *concrete*, *abstract*, or *collective* on the blanks beside the words.

1. vase _____

2. happiness _____

3. brood _____

4. orchestra _____

5. desk _____

6. loyalty _____

7. coin _____

8. trustees _____

9. friendship _____

10. enjoyment _____

B. Directions

List two *concrete* nouns, two *abstract* nouns, and two *collective* nouns.

NOUNS

Statement

A noun can be singular or plural. This is called *number*.

Singular—one
Plural—more than one

A. Directions

Label these nouns. Write *singular* or *plural* on the blanks beside the words.

1. brush   _____

2. stars   _____

3. boxes   _____

4. mitten   _____

5. berries   _____

6. marble   _____

7. shelves   _____

8. pony   _____

9. elf   _____

10. kings   _____

B. Directions

Write the plural form of the *singular* words above.

NOUNS

Statement

A noun's *gender* can be masculine, feminine, common, or neuter

Masculine—male
Feminine—female
Common—either male or female
Neuter—neither male nor female

A. Directions

Identify the gender of these nouns as *masculine, feminine, common,* or *neuter.*
Put an X in the correct column.

	masculine	feminine	common	neuter
1. girl				
2. foal				
3. singer				
4. boy				
5. box				
6. child				
7. teacher				
8. mother				
9. father				
10. glass				

B. Directions

List two *masculine,* two *feminine,* three *common,* and three *neuter* nouns.

NOUNS

Statement

A noun's *gender* can be masculine, feminine, common, or neuter.

A. Directions

Determine the gender of the underlined noun, and write *m, f, c,* or *n* on the blanks before the sentences.

_____ 1. A <u>monkey</u> swung through the trees.

_____ 2. Some <u>pieces</u> of the puzzle were missing.

_____ 3. <u>Mark Twain</u> was a famous humorist.

_____ 4. The <u>king</u> rode his horse in the parade.

_____ 5. The <u>baby</u> held the rattle tightly.

_____ 6. <u>Emily Dickinson</u> wrote many poems.

_____ 7. That kitchen <u>window</u> was cracked.

_____ 8. <u>Marie Curie</u> won a Nobel prize in physics.

_____ 9. <u>Sol</u> is another name for sun.

_____ 10. Those drama <u>students</u> attended the performance.

B. Directions

Write eight sentences—two with *masculine* nouns, two with *feminine* nouns, two with *common* nouns, and two with *neuter* nouns.

NOUNS

1. What is a noun?_____

2. _____ nouns are capitalized, and _____ nouns are not.

3. Nouns that name qualities or ideas are _____ nouns.

4. Nouns that name things one can see or touch are _____ nouns.

5. Nouns that name a group of people, animals, or things that are thought of as a unit are _____ nouns.

6. A noun can be _____ or _____ in number.

7. The simplest way to form a plural noun is to _____ to the singular.

   If the base word ends in a sibilant sound, form the plural by adding _____.

   If the base word ends in _y_ after a consonant, form the plural by changing the _____ to _____ and adding _____.

8. Form the plural of these words:

   torch   _____   mile   _____

   army   _____   city   _____

   book   _____   wish   _____

   duty   _____   light   _____

9. Masculine, feminine, common, and neuter refer to _____.

10. Identify the gender of these nouns:

   _____ uncle   _____ dog

   _____ mare   _____ grandpa

   _____ pencil   _____ aunt

   _____ fox   _____ chair

PRONOUNS

Statement

A *pronoun* takes the place of a noun.

A. Directions

Copy the following sentences, substitute a *pronoun* for the underlined word or words, and underline the pronoun.

1. <u>Justin</u> addressed the letter to <u>Alex</u>.

2. "Is <u>the pen</u> <u>Jill's</u>?" <u>Jill</u> asked.

3. <u>Sally</u> invited <u>Rosa</u> to the party.

4. "Tom, <u>Tom</u> may eat the last cupcake," said <u>Tom's</u> mother.

5. When will <u>Jane and LaShonda</u> return?

6. "<u>The mirror</u> belongs to <u>Eva</u>," said Nan.

7. <u>Leroy</u> gave the gifts to <u>Andy and Larry</u>.

8. <u>The bell's</u> tone was loud and clear.

9. Are the books <u>Cathy's and Rachel's</u>?

10. "Leo will type the report for <u>Roy and Mark</u>," announced Roy and Mark.

B. Directions

Write two sentences and underline the nouns. Copy the sentences and substitute pronouns for the underlined nouns. Underline the pronouns.

PRONOUNS

Statement

A *pronoun* takes the place of a noun.

A. Directions

Underline the *pronouns* in these sentences.

1. I took the matches from him.

2. Did he find the keys?

3. You inquired about it last week.

4. Is the scarf yours or hers?

5. The candy is mine.

6. We will not know until they tell us.

7. She asked me, "Are these ours?"

8. My mother selected them.

9. The dog wagged its tail.

10. Whose coat did she borrow?

B. Directions

Write three sentences using pronouns. Underline the pronouns.

PRONOUNS

Statement

A *pronoun* takes the place of a noun.

Personal pronouns refer to people.
Interrogative pronouns ask questions.
Demonstrative pronouns point out definite people or things.
Indefinite pronouns do not refer to definite people or things.
Relative pronouns introduce clauses that refer to another word in the sentence.

A. Directions

Identify the underlined pronouns. Write *personal, interrogative, demonstrative, indefinite,* or *relative* on the blanks before the sentences.

_____ 1. <u>Who</u> found the book?

_____ 2. <u>I</u> baked cookies for <u>him</u>.

_____

_____ 3. The dog <u>that</u> barked at <u>us</u> wore a red collar.

_____

_____ 4. <u>This</u> is the right way.

_____ 5. <u>What</u> was the question?

_____ 6. Did <u>anyone</u> ask for <u>me</u>?

_____

_____ 7. <u>Everybody</u> enjoyed the concert.

_____ 8. Bess, <u>whom</u> <u>you</u> met at the party, will be in the class.

_____

_____ 9. <u>Those</u> were left on the counter.

_____ 10. <u>Someone</u> called <u>them</u> from the station.

_____

B. Directions

List two examples of each kind of pronoun.

PRONOUNS

Statement

A *pronoun* takes the place of a noun.

> Personal pronouns refer to people.
> Interrogative pronouns ask questions.
> Demonstrative pronouns point out definite people or things.
> Indefinite pronouns do not refer to definite people or things.
> Relative pronouns introduce clauses that refer to another word in the sentence.

A. Directions

Identify the underlined pronouns. Write *personal, interrogative, demonstrative, indefinite,* or *relative* on the blanks before the sentences.

_____ 1. <u>She</u> will feed the puppy after class.

_____ 2. Ellen, <u>who</u> baked the cake, arrived at three.

_____ 3. <u>These</u> were packed in dry ice.

_____ 4. <u>Who</u> is Bob's teacher?

_____ 5. <u>Somebody</u> left the coat on the bench.

_____ 6. <u>We</u> mailed the letter before noon.

_____ 7. <u>That</u> is the largest box.

_____ 8. <u>Whom</u> did <u>they</u> elect?

_____

_____ 9. <u>Anyone</u> can attend the concert.

_____ 10. Henry read the book <u>that</u> was on the table.

B. Directions

Write five sentences—one with a *personal* pronoun, one with an *interrogative* pronoun, one with a *demonstrative* pronoun, one with an *indefinite* pronoun, and one with a *relative* pronoun.

PRONOUNS

Statement

A *noun* is the name of a person, place, thing, or idea.

A *pronoun* takes the place of a noun.

A. Directions

Underline the *nouns* and *pronouns* in these sentences. Write *n.* above the nouns and *pron.* above the pronouns.

1. We sat in the balcony at the theater.

2. She held the packages for Mara.

3. They waited for him at the corner.

4. Ben will tell you about the circus.

5. He brought the tickets to us at noon.

6. You will find the books on the desk.

7. Jordan collects hats, and he wears them often.

8. If anyone finds the key, give it to her before she leaves the office.

9. These are not mine.

10. Who will drive for him?

B. Directions

Write two sentences; use a noun and a pronoun in each sentence. Label the nouns and pronouns.

PRONOUNS

1. A _____ takes the place of a noun.

2. The five kinds of pronouns are _____ ,

   _____ , _____ ,

   _____ , and _____ .

3. _____ pronouns refer to persons.

4. _____ pronouns are words used to ask questions.

5. _____ pronouns point out definite people or things.

6. _____ pronouns do not refer to definite people or things.

7. _____ pronouns introduce clauses that refer to another word in the sentence.

8. First person is the person _____.

   Second person is the person _____.

   Third person is the person _____.

9. Compound personal pronouns are formed by adding

   _____ or _____ to personal pronouns.

10. Compound personal pronouns can be _____ or

    _____ pronouns.

11. A_____ pronoun refers back to the subject.

    An _____ pronoun is used for emphasis.

12. Relative pronouns relate to preceding nouns. The word to which the pronoun refers is the _____ .

13. If the antecedent is the name of a person, use _____ .

    If the antecedent is the name of a thing and is followed by a nonrestrictive clause, use _____ .

    If the antecedent is the name of a person or thing and is followed by a restrictive clause, use

    _____ .

    The word _____ refers to an idea and does not have an antecedent.

14. Singular means _____ . Plural means

    _____ .

15. Plurals of pronouns are formed differently than plurals of nouns.

    Pronouns change _____ .

16. Masculine, feminine, and neuter refer to _____ .

17. Nouns do not change form to show person as pronouns do. Nouns are usually the person spoken about or _____ . Nouns showing the person spoken to, or _____ , are nouns in direct address.

VERBS

Statement

A *verb* is a word that shows action or state of being. An *action verb* tells what something does.

A verb can show
physical action—run, sing, rest
mental action—remember, think, wish

A. Directions

Underline the *action verbs*.

1. Ming found a dime on the ground.

2. Troy predicts rain.

3. We went to the zoo last Friday.

4. Joan and her classmates rode the Ferris wheel.

5. Ms. Ross met the students at the picnic site.

6. Tom plays chess at the club.

7. Sherry and Austin chased butterflies.

8. Grace washed the dishes.

9. Frank picked tulips.

10. Tigers roared loudly.

B. Directions

Write three sentences using action verbs. Underline the action verbs.

VERBS

Statement

State of being verbs are called linking verbs because they connect or *link* a word in the predicate to the subject.

Linking verbs are

1. forms of the verb *to be—is, are, was, were*
2. verbs of the senses—*see, hear, taste, smell, feel*
3. sometimes the words—*look, seem, grow, appear*

A. Directions

Underline the *linking verbs.*

1. Those apples are red.

2. The package seems light.

3. This surface is smooth.

4. The lilacs smell pleasant.

5. A lemon tastes sour.

6. That story was interesting.

7. The weeds look tall.

8. I am happy now.

9. The blanket feels soft.

10. The music sounds loud.

B. Directions

Write three sentences using linking verbs. Underline the linking verbs.

VERBS

Statement

An *auxiliary verb* is a helping verb. It helps the main verb in the sentence. The auxiliary verb may be separated from the main verb in the sentence.

A. Directions

Underline the *main verb* and the *helping verb(s)* in each sentence.

1. The farmer is planting corn.

2. May I collect shells now?

3. The bells will ring at seven o'clock.

4. I am going now.

5. Chores should have been finished before six.

6. Have they counted the votes yet?

7. Did Lee return the ticket?

8. You could call her in the morning.

9. That dog has barked continuously.

10. He must have sold the most candy.

B. Directions

Write three sentences using auxiliary verbs. Underline the main verb and auxiliary verbs.

VERBS

Statement

A *verb* shows action or state of being.
An *action verb* shows action.
A *linking verb* links something in the predicate to the subject.
An *auxiliary verb* is a helping verb.

A. Directions

Underline the verbs. Label them as *action*, *linking*, or *auxiliary* on the blanks before the sentences. Three sentences have two-word verbs.

_____ 1. Huge waves pounded the shore.

_____ 2. That light has flashed for ten minutes.

_____

_____ 3. Homemade bread smells delicious.

_____ 4. Music soothes the fretful baby.

_____ 5. Jumbo, the elephant, was enormous.

_____ 6. Have those bears eaten food?

_____

_____ 7. Snowflakes swirled dizzily through the air.

_____ 8. The cat purred softly.

_____ 9. This bread is stale.

_____ 10. Had the tides risen dangerously?

_____

B. Directions

Write three sentences. Use an action verb, a linking verb, and an auxiliary verb.

VERBS

Statement

A *verb* either tells what the subject is doing or provides information about the state or condition of the subject. A verb must agree with the subject in number.

Singular subject—singular verb
Plural subject—plural verb

A. Directions

Identify these subjects and verbs as *singular* or *plural*.

1. Umpire decides   _____

2. Goblets glisten   _____

3. Thimble protects   _____

4. Eagles soar   _____

5. Whippets race   _____

6. Skaters glide   _____

7. Volunteer helps   _____

8. Star twinkles   _____

9. Bears hibernate   _____

10. Fire crackles   _____

B. Directions

Write four sentences. Use a singular subject and verb in two sentences, and a plural subject and verb in two sentences.

VERBS

Statement

There are two kinds of verbs—*transitive* and *intransitive*.

A *transitive verb* has a receiver of the action.
An *intransitive verb* has no receiver of the action.

A. Directions

Underline the verbs. Write a *t* in the blank if the verb is *transitive* or an *i* if the verb is *intransitive*.

_____ 1. The farmer planted corn in the large field.

_____ 2. We will be at the party tonight.

_____ 3. Dictionaries were placed on the desks.

_____ 4. David baked a lemon pie.

_____ 5. The author sharpened the yellow pencil.

_____ 6. Sherlock Holmes looked for clues in each room.

_____ 7. It was a very interesting book.

_____ 8. The supplies were ordered last week.

_____ 9. They meet for lunch everyday.

_____ 10. The program was planned by Lucy.

B. Directions

Write four sentences. Use transitive verbs in two sentences and intransitive verbs in two sentences. Underline the verbs, and label them.

VERBS

Statement

A transitive verb has a receiver of the action. If the subject acts and the object receives the action, the verb is in the *active* voice.

If the subject receives the action, the verb is in the *passive voice*.

A. Directions

Underline the *verbs*. Write an *a* in the blank if the verb is in the *active voice* or a *p* if the verb is in the *passive voice*.

_____   1. Brandon purchased the tickets.

_____   2. Letters have been sent to all participants by the committee.

_____   3. A toll was collected by the attendant in the booth.

_____   4. The girl fixed her bike.

_____   5. The poems were written by the students.

_____   6. That car was driven by the winner.

_____   7. Sunshine melted the snowman.

_____   8. Mother set the basket of fruit on the table.

_____   9. The cake was decorated by Max.

_____   10. Children enjoyed the clown's antics.

B. Directions

Write two sentences using the active voice and two sentences using the passive voice.

VERBS

Statement

Only transitive verbs (verbs that have a receiver of the action) have voice. An intransitive verb has no receiver of the action. A transitive verb is in the *active voice* if the subject does the acting. If the subject receives the action, the verb is in the *passive voice*.

An auxiliary verb, such as *have, has,* or *had,* helps to express an idea in the passive voice.

A. Directions

Underline the verbs. If the verb is *intransitive,* write an *i* in the blank. If the verb is *transitive,* write a *t* in the blank and either an *a* for *active voice* or a *p* for *passive voice.*

_____ 1. The caterer was hired last month.

_____ 2. Ann closed the door.

_____ 3. Did you set the flowers on the table?

_____ 4. They went to the beach last summer.

_____ 5. The children awoke at six o'clock on Christmas morning.

_____ 6. America was named for Amerigo Vespucci.

_____ 7. Edward took the blankets to them.

_____ 8. It was a delightful program.

_____ 9. Money was involved in that transaction.

_____ 10. Sue arrived early for the celebration.

B. Directions

Write three sentences. Use a transitive verb in active voice. Use a transitive verb in passive voice. Use an intransitive verb.

VERBS

Statement

Only transitive verbs (verbs that have a receiver of the action) have voice. An intransitive verb has no receiver of the action. A transitive verb is in the *active voice* if the subject does the acting. If the subject receives the action, the verb is in the *passive voice*.

An auxiliary verb, such as *have*, *has*, or *had*, helps to express an idea in passive voice.

A. Directions

Underline the verbs. If the verb is *intransitive*, write an *i* in the blank. If the verb is *transitive*, write a *t* in the blank and either an *a* for *active voice* or a *p* for *passive voice*.

_____ 1. Plans have been made by the class.

_____ 2. That news was heard by a large audience.

_____ 3. They were waiting for the latest report.

_____ 4. He docked the boat before noon.

_____ 5. We sent for the doctor.

_____ 6. Will you string these beads?

_____ 7. Seth chuckled gleefully.

_____ 8. Did she pack her suitcase yesterday?

_____ 9. That subject was discussed in detail.

_____ 10. I will wait for an explanation.

B. Directions

Write three sentences. Use a transitive verb in active voice. Use a transitive verb in passive voice. Use an intransitive verb.

VERBS

Statement

The three *principal parts* of a *verb* are present, past, and past participle.

The past and past participle of *regular verbs* are formed by adding *-ed* to the present tense.

The past and past participle of *irregular verbs* are formed by changing a vowel or the form of the verb. Sometimes the form remains the same for all the parts. If you are unsure of a verb's form, consult a dictionary.

A. Directions

Write the principal parts of the following verbs.

PRESENT	PAST	PAST PARTICIPLE
1. help	_____	_____
2. take	_____	_____
3. run	_____	_____
4. shop	_____	_____
5. play	_____	_____
6. fly	_____	_____
7. bake	_____	_____
8. drink	_____	_____
9. change	_____	_____
10. give	_____	_____

VERBS

Statement

Tense expresses when the action takes place.

A. Directions

Underline the verb in each sentence, and identify the tense—*present, past,* or *future.*

_____   1. The plumber will install the new dishwasher tomorrow.

_____   2. A white rabbit hopped across the meadow.

_____   3. The palomino trots around the ring.

_____   4. We shall begin construction next week.

_____   5. The accountant figured her tax early.

_____   6. That beagle barks at strangers.

_____   7. She will bring sandwiches to the skating party.

_____   8. They jog every morning.

_____   9. The sound reverberates through the hall.

_____   10. He will review the material before taking the test.

B. Directions

Write three sentences—one with the verb *burn* in the present tense, one with the verb *ring* in the past tense, and one with the verb *broil* in the future tense. Underline the verbs.

VERBS

Statement

Tense expresses when the action takes place.

A. Directions

Underline the verb in each sentence, and identify the tense—*present perfect*, *past perfect*, or *future perfect*.

_____ 1. They have driven to Atlanta many times.

_____ 2. We had parked the car across the street.

_____ 3. Marcus will have returned the tape before the seventh of June.

_____ 4. He will have finished the assignment before Sunday.

_____ 5. She has asked that question repeatedly.

_____ 6. The wind had blown all the leaves from the tree.

_____ 7. Kevin will have collected the fee before the meeting.

_____ 8. I have studied the map.

_____ 9. Dawn had mowed the lawn on Saturday.

_____ 10. The weatherman had predicted snow.

B. Directions

Write three sentences—one with the verb *win* in the present perfect tense, one with the verb *eat* in the past perfect tense, and one with the verb *call* in the future perfect tense. Underline the verbs.

VERBS

Statement

When choosing the correct form of troublesome verbs, it is helpful to refer to the verb's definition.

Lie:	to recline	Lay:	to place
Sit:	to rest	Set:	to place
Rise:	to get up	Raise:	to lift

A. Directions

For each sentence choose the correct form of the verb in parentheses, and fill in the blank.

1. He _____ the pot on the stove.
   (past tense sit/set)

2. She _____ on the raft in the pool.
   (present tense lie/lay)

3. He _____ before six o'clock every morning.
   (future tense rise/raise)

4. Smoke _____ from the chimney.
   (past tense rise/raise)

5. The librarian _____ that book on the cart yesterday.
   (past perfect tense lie/lay)

6. They _____ in the third row for the last three games.
   (present perfect tense sit/set)

7. The moon _____ before the party ends.
   (future perfect tense rise/raise)

8. He _____ the flag to the top of the staff.
   (past tense rise/raise)

9. _____ the sweater on the bed before you go.
   (present tense lie/lay)

10. She _____ on the stage to introduce the speaker.
    (present tense sit/set)

B. Directions

Write six sentences. Use the verb *raise* in the present tense, the verb *set* in the past tense, the verb *lie* in the future tense, the verb *lay* in the present perfect tense, the verb *rise* in the past perfect tense, and the verb *sit* in the future perfect tense.

VERBS

Statement

Mood describes the way a statement is expressed.

> *Indicative* is used to state a fact or ask a question.
> *Imperative* is used to express a command.
> *Subjunctive* is used to express a wish or a condition contrary to fact.

A. Directions

The verbs in these sentences are in the subjunctive mood.

On the blank before each sentence, write *wish* or *contrary to fact.*

_____ 1. If she were older, she would be eligible to enter the contest.

_____ 2. He wishes he were taller.

_____ 3. I wish I were a better skater.

_____ 4. If the book were longer, we couldn't have finished it.

_____ 5. She wishes she were older.

_____ 6. If they were listed, she wouldn't have forgotten the candles.

_____ 7. If you were there earlier, you wouldn't have missed the plane.

_____ 8. If the tickets were not so expensive, we could have gone to the concert.

_____ 9. I wish she were on my team.

_____ 10. I wish I were able to type faster.

B. Directions

Write four sentences in the subjunctive mood—two wishes and two statements that are contrary to fact.

VERBALS—PARTICIPLES, GERUNDS, INFINITIVES

Statement

Participles, *gerunds*, and *infinitives* are verb forms that are used as other parts of speech.

Participles function as adjectives.
Gerunds function as nouns.
Infinitives may be used as nouns, adjectives, or adverbs, and they are usually preceded by the word *to*.

A. Directions

Write *participle*, *gerund*, or *infinitive* on the blank before each sentence.

_____ 1. Scurrying into the hole, the mouse avoided the cat.

_____ 2. Skiing is their favorite sport.

_____ 3. We were determined to succeed.

_____ 4. Standing by the bridge, Horatius battled the Etruscans.

_____ 5. To raise sweet corn was her idea.

_____ 6. Shoveling snow was Don's regular winter chore.

_____ 7. Those students hope to graduate in the spring.

_____ 8. Opening the door, he saw definite signs of the blizzard.

_____ 9. Her wish was to dance.

_____ 10. Peeling apples was a boring task.

B. Directions

Write three sentences. Use a participle, a gerund, and an infinitive.

VERBS

1. A verb shows _____ or _____ .

2. A _____ connects or links a word in the predicate to the subject of the sentence.

3. Words used as linking verbs are forms of the verb _____ and verbs of the _____ . The words *look*, *seem*, *grow*, and *appear* are also used as _____ .

4. An _____ verb is a helping verb. It helps the _____ verb.

5. A _____ verb has a receiver of the action. An _____ verb does not have a receiver of the action.

6. Only transitive verbs have _____ . When the subject does the acting, the verb is in the _____ voice. When the subject receives the action, the verb is in the _____ voice.

7. _____ expresses when the action takes place.

8. The six tenses are _____ , _____ , _____ , _____ , _____ , and _____ .

9. First person refers to the person _____ , second person refers to the person _____ , and third person refers to the person _____ .

10. The subjunctive mood is used to express a _____ or a
_____ .

11. Most verbs have three basic forms. They are _____ ,
_____ , and _____ .

12. Many verbs form the past tense and past participle by adding
_____ to the present tense.

13. Some irregular verbs form the past tense and past participle by changing a
_____ or by changing the _____ of the verb.
Sometimes the form remains the _____ for all the parts.

14. The present participle is formed by adding _____ to the present
tense.

15. The perfect tenses are formed by adding the helping words _____ ,
_____ , _____ , or _____
to the past participle.

16. A list of a verb's forms is called _____ .

17. Define these troublesome verbs.

lie = _____   lay = _____

sit = _____   set = _____

rise = _____   raise = _____

18. A verb form that functions as an adjective is a _____ .

19. A verb form ending in *-ing* and used as a noun is a _____ .

20. A verb form used as a noun, an adjective, or an adverb and usually preceded by the
word *to* is an _____ .

ADJECTIVES

Statement

Adjectives modify nouns or pronouns. They describe (tell what kind), limit (tell how many), or point out information (tell which ones).

A. Directions

Underline the *nouns* in the sentences. Write *adj.* above the adjectives.

1. The big dog barked loudly.

2. A yellow bird sang cheerily.

3. Five students waited for the bus.

4. This book has ninety pages.

5. An oblong box contained the clips.

6. Several students baked the cookies.

7. That man collected the tickets.

8. The rusty nail was bent.

9. Many actors wanted the part in the play.

10. The muddy river flowed slowly.

B. Directions

Write three sentences. Use an adjective that describes, an adjective that limits, and an adjective that points out. Underline the nouns once and write *adj.* above the adjectives.

ADJECTIVES

Statement

Adjectives modify nouns or pronouns. They describe (tell color, size, shape, or kind), limit (tell number or quantity), or point out information (tell which ones).

A. Directions

Write *adj.* above the adjectives. On the blanks before the sentences, write whether the adjectives *describe*, *limit*, or *point out*.

_____ 1. The big dog barked loudly.

_____ 2. A yellow bird sang cheerily.

_____ 3. Five students waited for the bus.

_____ 4. This book has ninety pages.

_____ 5. An oblong box contained the clips.

_____ 6. Several students baked the cookies.

_____ 7. That man collected the tickets.

_____ 8. The rusty nail was bent.

_____ 9. Many actors wanted the part in the play.

_____ 10. The muddy river flowed slowly.

B. Directions

Write three sentences. Write *adj.* above the adjectives. Tell whether each adjective describes, limits, or points out.

ADJECTIVES

Statement

Adjectives have three degrees of comparison:

1. *Positive*   simple quality
2. *Comparative*   more quality
3. *Superlative*   most quality

There are three ways to change an adjective's degree of comparison:

1. Add *-er* or *-est*
2. Add *more* or *most*
3. Change its form

A. Directions

Write *adj.* above the adjectives. On the blanks before the sentences, write the degree of comparison—*positive, comparative,* or *superlative.*

_____   1. Ann has blue eyes.

_____   2. Amber's eyes are bluer.

_____   3. Quentin's eyes are the bluest.

_____   4. This is a good story.

_____   5. He wrote a better story.

_____   6. Bert wrote the best story.

_____   7. Jumbo was the biggest elephant.

_____   8. Lee's puzzle is difficult.

_____   9. My puzzle is more difficult.

_____   10. Lena's puzzle is the most difficult.

B. Directions

Write three sentences using the three degrees of comparison—positive, comparative, and superlative.

ADJECTIVES—NOUNS—VERBS

Statement

Adjectives modify nouns. They describe, limit, or point out information about the noun.

Nouns name a person, place, thing, or idea. They are common or proper.

Verbs show action or state of being. There are action verbs, linking verbs, and auxiliary verbs.

A. Directions

Write *adj.* above the adjectives. Underline the nouns once and the verbs twice.

1. Bernardo wore rimless glasses.

2. The chef used seedless grapes in the salad.

3. A young lady sat in the comfortable chair.

4. Hopeful contestants will await the decision.

5. Ruben flipped the shiny coin.

6. The area was enclosed with a wooden fence.

7. An industrious worker has arrived early.

8. The reddish cast of the sky worried the sailors.

9. Chicago is a large city.

10. Anna Pavlova was a famous dancer.

B. Directions

Write three sentences. Write *adj.* above the adjectives. Underline the nouns once and the verbs twice.

ADJECTIVES

Statement

Adjectives modify nouns. They describe, limit, or point out information about a noun.

A. Directions

Write *adj.* above the adjectives.

1. Those balloons were filled with helium.

2. The unhappy man hung the bright shawl on the wooden peg.

3. She loaded twelve boxes on the large cart.

4. The yellow pear is ripe.

5. The kind doctor examined the nervous patient.

6. A little French boy sailed a white boat in the blue pool.

7. Three ducks waddled across the green lawn.

8. She is slow and careful.

9. Heavy tanks lumbered across the hot desert sand.

10. The wind is cold and damp.

B. Directions

Write three sentences. Use adjectives that describe, limit, and point out. Write *adj.* above the adjectives.

ADJECTIVES

1. An _____ modifies a noun or pronoun.

2. Adjectives _____ , _____ , or _____ information about a noun or pronoun.

3. Adjectives that describe tell _____ , _____ , _____ , or _____ .

4. Adjectives that limit tell the _____ or _____ .

5. Adjectives that point out tell _____ .

6. The three degrees of comparison of adjectives are _____ , _____ , and _____ .

7. To form the comparative and superlative degrees of one-syllable words, add _____ and _____ to the positive degree.

8. To form the comparative and superlative degrees of words of more than one-syllable, add _____ and _____ to the positive degree.

9. To form the comparative and superlative degrees of some adjectives, change their _____ .

10. When adjectives are subject complements and follow a linking verb, they are called _____ .

ADVERBS

Statement

Adverbs modify verbs, adjectives, or other adverbs. They tell how, when, where, or to what extent.

A. Directions

Underline the verbs twice. Write *adv.* above the adverbs. On the blanks before the sentences, write what the adverb tells about the verb—*how, when, where,* or *to what extent.*

_____ 1. The band practiced downstairs.

_____ 2. Amy called twice.

_____ 3. He acted foolishly.

_____ 4. My sister will arrive soon.

_____ 5. John plays well.

_____ 6. Kristen danced gracefully across the stage.

_____ 7. Chris watched the players intently.

_____ 8. When will Jack finish the project?

_____ 9. A cannon boomed loudly.

_____ 10. Dan will be there.

B. Directions

Write four sentences. Use adverbs that modify verbs and tell how, when, where, or to what extent. Underline the verbs twice. Write *adv.* above each adverb. Then after each sentence, describe the adverb by writing *how, when, where,* or *to what extent.*

ADVERBS

Statement

Adverbs modify verbs, adjectives, or other adverbs. They tell how, when, where, or to what extent.

A. Directions

Write *adv.* above the adverbs in the sentences below. On the blank before each sentence, identify the part of speech of the word that the adverb modifies by writing *v.*, *adj.*, or *adv.*

_____ 1. The train sped rapidly through the tunnel.

_____ 2. Was that statement really true?

_____ 3. They will be very late.

_____ 4. The violinist played extremely well.

_____ 5. That concert was very good.

_____ 6. Bill made the announcement carefully and distinctly.

_____ 7. Jamal spoke too rapidly.

_____ 8. We did not understand the directions.

_____ 9. The child was mysteriously quiet.

_____ 10. Those stones are exceedingly rare.

B. Directions

Write three sentences. Use adverbs to modify a verb, an adjective, and an adverb.

ADVERBS AND ADJECTIVES

Statement

Adjectives modify nouns. They describe, limit, or point out information about a noun.

Adverbs modify verbs, adjectives, or other adverbs. They tell how, when, where, or to what extent.

A. Directions

Write *adj.* above the adjectives and *adv.* above the adverbs in the sentences below.

1. The nervous child looked hopefully at the clock.

2. Where did you park the tan van?

3. A fat pig gobbled the corn greedily.

4. The boat sailed smoothly over the calm sea.

5. A red fox ran swiftly over the hill.

6. The skilled skater glided gracefully on the smooth ice.

7. A shrill siren wailed loudly.

8. Shy Mike seldom attends the meetings.

9. The brave team fearlessly faced defeat.

10. Have you ridden the new bus lately?

B. Directions

Write three sentences. Use an adjective and an adverb in each sentence. Write *adj.* above the adjectives and *adv.* above the adverbs.

ADVERBS AND ADJECTIVES

Statement

Adjectives modify nouns. They describe, limit, or point out information about a noun. Predicate adjectives are used after linking verbs or verbs of the senses.

Adverbs modify verbs, adjectives, or other adverbs. They tell how, when, where, or to what extent.

Reminders:

> *Good* is an adjective.
> *Well* is an adverb or a predicate adjective
> *Real* is an adjective.
> *Really* is an adverb.

A. Directions

Choose the correct word from the parentheses to fill in each blank.

1. Ron skis_____ . (good, well)

2. The syrup was _____ . (sweet, sweetly)

3. Brenda felt _____ because she was late. (bad, badly)

4. The actor played her roles_____ . (good, well)

5. She sang _____ . (sweet, sweetly)

6. Her perfume smells _____ . (good, well)

7. The history test was_____ . (easy, easily)

8. We won the contest _____ . (easy, easily)

9. The taffy tasted _____ . (good, well)

10. Matt was _____ careful when he delivered the package. (real, really)

11. "Are those _____ roses?" asked Stuart. (real, really)

12. She played _____ in the second half of the game. (bad, badly)

13. That movie star looked _____ , and she dressed

_____ .

(beautiful, beautifully)

14. I am _____ tired. (extreme, extremely)

B. Directions

Number your paper from 1 to 14, and write whether the answers from Part A are *adjectives* or *adverbs*.

PREPOSITIONS

Statement

Prepositions show the relationship of nouns or pronouns to other words in the sentence. The noun or pronoun is called the object of the preposition. The preposition and its object are called a prepositional phrase.

A. Directions

Circle the *prepositions* and write the *objects of the prepositions* on the blanks beside the phrases.

1. on the table   _____

2. over the hill   _____

3. in a box   _____

4. under the bridge   _____

5. around the corner   _____

6. across the street   _____

7. near the lake   _____

8. at the station   _____

9. beside the house   _____

10. through the woods   _____

B. Directions

Write five prepositional phrases.

PREPOSITIONS

Statement

Prepositions show the relationship of nouns or pronouns to other words in the sentence. The noun or pronoun is called the object of the preposition. The preposition and its object are called a prepositional phrase.

A. Directions

Underline the prepositional phrases. Write *prep.* above the prepositions and *obj. of prep.* above the objects of the prepositions.

1. Jerry walked over the slippery ice.

2. The ball bounced down the stairs.

3. A child ran through the house.

4. Nathan jumped off the step.

5. Ashley stood near them.

6. A ball landed in the sand.

7. The train chugged up the mountain.

8. He set the roses on the table.

9. Stephanie sang to the sleepy baby.

10. Linda tossed the ball through the hoop.

B. Directions

Write three sentences. Underline the prepositional phrases. Write *prep.* above the prepositions and *obj. of prep.* above the objects of the prepositions.

PREPOSITIONAL PHRASES

Statement

A preposition and its object are called a *prepositional phrase*. *Adjective prepositional phrases* modify nouns or pronouns. *Adverbial prepositional phrases* modify verbs, adjectives, or adverbs.

A. Directions

Underline the prepositional phrases. On the blanks before the sentences, write *adj.* if the phrases modify nouns or pronouns and *adv.* if they modify verbs, adjectives, or adverbs. Some sentences have more than one prepositional phrase.

_____ 1. The coat was hung behind the door.

_____ 2. The rain beat against the window.

_____ 3. That vase from China is priceless.

_____ 4. A bell in the tower rang at twelve o'clock.

_____ 5. She eased the car down the steep incline.

_____ 6. He anchored the boat near the shore.

_____ 7. A box under the bed was filled with blankets.

_____ 8. The liner from Le Havre docked at the pier.

_____ 9. They selected the apartment across the street.

_____ 10. The park within the city limits was the site for the picnic.

B. Directions

Write four sentences. Include two *adjective* prepositional phrases and two *adverbial* prepositional phrases.

Underline and label the prepositional phrases.

PREPOSITIONAL PHRASES

Statement

A preposition and its object are called a *prepositional phrase. Adjective prepositional phrases* modify nouns or pronouns.

Adverbial prepositional phrases modify verbs, adjectives, or adverbs.

A. Directions

Underline the prepositional phrases. On the blanks before the sentences, write *adj.* if the phrases modify nouns or pronouns and *adv.* if they modify verbs, adjectives, or adverbs. Some sentences have more than one prepositional phrase.

_____ 1. A small plane flew between the clouds.

_____ 2. Those shoes in the box are new.

_____ 3. Scoop the ice cream into another bowl.

_____ 4. The rumors about Daryl are untrue.

_____ 5. The jewels inside the vault were insured.

_____ 6. Keep the supplies beneath the sink.

_____ 7. Cans of food were placed in the barrel.

_____ 8. The house stands beyond that row of poplar trees.

_____ 9. We ate dinner after the movie.

_____ 10. Count the bicycles beside the school.

B. Directions

Write four sentences. Underline the prepositional phrases, and label them as *adjective* or *adverbial*.

CONJUNCTIONS

Statement

Conjunctions join or connect words or groups of words.
Coordinate conjunctions join words or clauses of equal value.
Subordinate conjunctions join clauses of unequal value.
Correlative conjunctions are used in pairs.

A. Directions

Underline the *conjunctions*.

1. Laura and Joan wrote the letters.

2. Greg and I finished the report by noon.

3. Henry will attend the meeting unless he is ill.

4. Neither Imelda nor Clara will be there.

5. Both Dale and Toya have won medals.

6. Because it rained, the picnic was cancelled.

7. He will ask either Martha or Tracy for the number.

8. The little dog was cold and hungry.

9. The puma crouched and sprung.

10. After Rex left, the mail arrived.

B. Directions

Number your paper from 1–10, and identify the types of conjunctions used in the sentences above. Remember that correlative conjunctions are used in pairs.

CONJUNCTIONS

Statement

Conjunctions join or connect words or groups of words.
Coordinate conjunctions join words or clauses of equal value.
Subordinate conjunctions join a dependent clause with an independent clause.
Correlative conjunctions are used in pairs.

A. Directions

Underline the *conjunctions*. On the blanks before the sentences, identify the conjunctions as *coordinate, subordinate,* or *correlative*.

_____ 1. Heather drew a picture, and Lorna wrote a poem.

_____ 2. That team hasn't won a game since Gail broke her legs.

_____ 3. Unless it stops raining, we won't go.

_____ 4. If you want to attend the fall class, you should enroll now.

_____ 5. The book was long, but the story was suspenseful.

_____ 6. As the orchestra played the last note, the crowd applauded.

_____ 7. Because the price was too high, Bill didn't buy the jacket.

_____ 8. Either Tina or Carla will teach the class.

_____ 9. Although he worked late, Jason didn't finish the typing.

_____ 10. Will they come to the restaurant, or will they meet us later at the theater?

B. Directions

Write three sentences. Use a *coordinate* conjunction, a *subordinate* conjunction, and *correlative* conjunctions. Underline the conjunctions, and label them.

ADVERBS, PREPOSITIONS, CONJUNCTIONS

1. An adverb describes or modifies a _____ , an _____ , or another _____ .

2. Adverbs answer the questions _____ , _____ , _____ , and _____ .

3. _____ is an adverb used as an interrupter.

4. Adverbs usually come _____ the verb.

5. Adverbs often end in _____ .

6. A _____ shows the relationship of nouns or pronouns to other words in the sentence.

7. A preposition and its _____ are called a prepositional phrase.

8. Adjective prepositional phrases modify _____ or _____ .

9. Adverbial prepositional phrases modify _____ , _____ , or _____ .

10. _____ join or connect words or groups of words.

11. _____ conjunctions join words or clauses of equal value.

_____ conjunctions join clauses of unequal value.

_____ conjunctions are used in pairs.

INTERJECTIONS

Statement

Interjections show strong feeling. They are not related grammatically to other words in the sentence.

A. Directions

Write the *interjections* on the blanks before the sentences.

_____ 1. Good! They arrived before the play started.

_____ 2. Hurrah! We are going to the parade.

_____ 3. Bravo! The performance was excellent.

_____ 4. Oh! Stop the toddler.

_____ 5. Whew! That was a close call.

_____ 6. Shoo! I can't discuss the plan now.

_____ 7. Alas! We were too late.

_____ 8. Bah! That report is not true.

_____ 9. Ugh! The medicine is bitter.

_____ 10. Whoa! We are going too fast.

B. Directions

Write three sentences. Use an interjection in each sentence. Underline the interjections, and punctuate them with an exclamation point.

INTERJECTIONS

Statement

Interjections show strong feeling. They are not related grammatically to other words in the sentence.

A. Directions

Underline the *interjections* in these sentences.

1. Whew! I'm very tired.

2. Ouch! Don't touch my sunburn.

3. Ha! Anyone can answer that question.

4. Enough! I can't believe that.

5. Aha! That team made two more points.

6. Yikes! That movie was terrible.

7. Well! When are you going to pay that bill?

8. Hey! Watch where you are going.

9. Ah! Chocolate souffle tastes so good.

10. Good! I'll recommend him to the chef.

B. Directions

Write three sentences. Use an interjection in each sentence. Underline the interjections, and punctuate them with an exclamation point.

SENTENCE OR FRAGMENT

Statement

A *sentence* has a subject and a predicate and expresses a complete thought.

A *fragment* is an incomplete statement.

A. Directions

On the blanks, write *s* before each sentence, and put an *x* before each fragment.

_____	1. around the corner
_____	2. the frisky puppy bit the slipper
_____	3. tom sang a happy tune
_____	4. ribbons in the box
_____	5. the rain fell in torrents
_____	6. a clown in a purple vest
_____	7. morgan toasted marshmallows
_____	8. soared high above the clouds
_____	9. was adorned with sequins
_____	10. jeff stacked the books on the third shelf

B. Directions

Copy the sentences from Part A. Underline the subject once and the verb twice.

Add subjects and predicates to the fragments from Part A, so they express complete thoughts. Underline the subject once and the verb twice.

SENTENCE OR FRAGMENT

Statement

A *sentence* has a subject and a predicate and expresses a complete thought.

A *fragment* is an incomplete statement.

A. Directions

On the blanks, write *s* before each sentence, and put an *x* before each fragment.

_____ 1. whales are huge mammals

_____ 2. an elephant's trunk

_____ 3. the last slice of chocolate cake

_____ 4. the farmer milked the cow

_____ 5. that clown's antics were funny

_____ 6. from the case

_____ 7. charles enjoyed the concert

_____ 8. the moon in the sky

_____ 9. whitecaps on the lake

_____ 10. the ballerinas danced to the music from *Swan Lake*

B. Directions

Copy the sentences from Part A. Underline the subject once and the verb twice.

Add subjects and predicates to the fragments from Part A, so they express complete thoughts. Underline the subject once and the verb twice.

TYPES OF SENTENCES

Statement

Sentences begin with capital letters. The end punctuation is determined by the thought expressed. There are four kinds of sentences.

1. *Declarative* sentences state facts. They are punctuated with a period.
2. *Interrogative* sentences ask questions. They are punctuated with a question mark.
3. *Imperative* sentences make requests or commands. They are punctuated with a period.
4. *Exclamatory* sentences express strong feelings. They are punctuated with an exclamation point.

A. Directions

Write *declarative, interrogative, imperative,* or *exclamatory* on the blank before each sentence.

_____   1. Mail those letters before noon.

_____   2. Hurry! The fire is spreading!

_____   3. Will Sally mail the package before the seventeenth?

_____   4. Raindrops pelted the tin roof.

_____   5. Has the plane arrived at the gate?

_____   6. Close both doors.

_____   7. The snow was deep.

_____   8. Shall I add lemon flavor to the icing?

_____   9. Help! I have fallen!

_____   10. Is the store open at night?

B. Directions

Write and correctly punctuate one *declarative,* one *imperative,* one *exclamatory,* and one *interrogative* sentence.

SENTENCES

Statement

Sentences begin with capital letters. The end punctuation is determined by the thought expressed. There are four kinds of sentences.

1. *Declarative* sentences state facts. They are punctuated with a period.
2. *Interrogative* sentences ask questions. They are punctuated with a question mark.
3. *Imperative* sentences make requests or commands. They are punctuated with a period.
4. *Exclamatory* sentences express strong feelings. They are punctuated with an exclamation point.

A. *Directions*

Punctuate the following sentences. Write *declarative, interrogative, imperative,* or *exclamatory* on the blank before each sentence.

_____ 1. Did Bill win the race

_____ 2. Tara will meet us at the mall

_____ 3. This plate is hot

_____ 4. Prepare the list before five o'clock

_____ 5. Will Dan drive to the airport

_____ 6. It's too late, Gina

_____ 7. Maria made date bars

_____ 8. Water the plants, Anna

_____ 9. A tornado is approaching

_____ 10. When was this book published

B. *Directions*

Write and correctly punctuate one *declarative*, one *interrogative*, one *imperative*, and one *exclamatory* sentence.

SENTENCES—SUBJECT AND PREDICATE

Statement

Every sentence has two parts—a *subject* and a *predicate*. The simple subject is a noun or a pronoun about which something is said. The simple predicate is a verb. It tells what the subject does (action verb), or it links something to the subject (linking verb).

A. Directions

Underline the simple subject once and the simple predicate twice.

1. Those students gave flowers to the teacher.

2. The boys returned the books before lunch.

3. The American flag is red, white, and blue.

4. Those muffins taste sweet.

5. A thirsty dog lapped water from the dish.

6. That music became too loud.

7. Ellen sang a solo at the concert.

8. The test was difficult.

9. The referee blew the whistle.

10. The lights are bright.

B. Directions

List three simple subjects and three simple predicates.

SENTENCES—SUBJECT AND PREDICATE

Statement

Every sentence has two parts—a *subject* and a *predicate.* The simple subject is a noun or a pronoun about which something is said. The simple predicate is a verb. It tells what the subject does (action verb), or it links something to the subject (linking verb).

A. Directions

Underline the simple subject once and the simple predicate twice.

1. Hot water boils rapidly.

2. The loud siren wailed eerily.

3. The red ball bounces high.

4. A gray elephant lumbered slowly into the jungle.

5. Sweet music gradually lulled the tired campers to sleep.

6. The bright sun rises early.

7. The professional golfer putts expertly.

8. Spanish castanets clicked rhythmically.

9. A yellow flame flickers softly.

10. Grape soda fizzed effervescently in the glass.

B. Directions

Write three sentences. Underline the simple subject once and the simple predicate twice.

SENTENCES—SUBJECT AND VERB AGREEMENT

Statement

A subject and verb must agree in number. A singular subject takes a singular verb. Most singular verbs end with one *s*.

EXAMPLE: pan shines

A plural subject takes a plural verb.
Most verbs that do **not** end with a single *s* are plural.

EXAMPLE: pans shine

Remember: This is the opposite for nouns; singular nouns do not usually end with a single *s*. Plural nouns usually do end with a single *s*.

A. Directions

Decide if the subject is singular or plural. Choose the correct verb form, and write it on the blank beside the word.

1. Dog   _____   (bark, barks)

2. Tops   _____   (spin, spins)

3. Baby   _____   (smile, smiles)

4. Wheel   _____   (turn, turns)

5. Nomad   _____   (wander, wanders)

6. Farmers   _____   (plow, plows)

7. Pans   _____   (shine, shines)

8. Hunter   _____   (shoot, shoots)

9. Lions   _____   (roar, roars)

10. Tulips   _____   (bloom, blooms)

B. Directions

List two singular subjects and singular verbs. List two plural subjects and plural verbs.

SENTENCES—ADJECTIVES AND ADVERBS

Statement

A sentence is made up of a subject, a predicate, and words that modify the subject and predicate.

Adjectives modify nouns or pronouns. They describe, limit, or point out information.

Adverbs modify verbs, adjectives, or adverbs. They tell how, when, where, or to what extent.

A. Directions

Write *adj.* above the adjectives and *adv.* above the adverbs in the sentences below.

1. Hot water boils rapidly.

2. The loud siren wailed eerily.

3. The red ball bounces high.

4. A gray elephant lumbered slowly into the jungle.

5. Sweet music gradually lulled the tired campers to sleep.

6. The bright sun rises early.

7. The professional golfer putts expertly.

8. Spanish castanets clicked rhythmically.

9. A yellow flame flickers softly.

10. Grape soda fizzed effervescently into the glass.

B. Directions

Write two sentences. Use a noun, a verb, an adjective, and an adverb in each sentence.

SENTENCES—DIAGRAMS

Statement

A *diagram* is a drawing that explains the structure of a sentence.

A. *Directions*

Diagram the sentences.

Show the simple subject and the simple predicate.

subject	predicate
(noun or pronoun)	(verb)

1. The boy ate cake.

2. Those horses were fast.

3. The leader dropped the baton.

4. Kendra was the president.

5. We popped the corn.

6. Apples are good.

7. I read the book.

8. Max selected the program.

9. The girl played the drums.

10. The baby is happy.

B. *Directions*

Write and then diagram two sentences. Show the simple subject and the simple predicate.

SENTENCES—DIAGRAMS

Statement

A *diagram* is a drawing that explains the structure of a sentence.

A. Directions

Diagram the sentences.

Show the subject, the action verb, and the direct object.

subject	action verb	direct object

1. The boy ate the cake.

2. The student completed the assignment.

3. The leader dropped the baton.

4. The waiter served the dessert.

5. We popped the corn.

6. The hunters chased the fox.

7. I read the book.

8. Max selected the program.

9. The girl played the drums.

10. Lightning struck the barn.

B. Directions

Write and then diagram two sentences. Show the subject, the action verb, and the direct object.

SENTENCES—DIAGRAMS

Statement

A *diagram* is a drawing that explains the structure of a sentence.

A. Directions

Diagram the sentences.

Show the subject, the linking verb, and the predicate nominative.

subject	linking verb	predicate nominative
(noun or pronoun)		(noun)

1. Terry was the president.

2. They are the editors.

3. He became the winner.

4. I am a student.

5. Chandra is my friend.

6. Boston is the capital.

7. Acorns become trees.

8. Edison and Bell were inventors.

9. The girls are dancers.

10. Texas is the Lone Star State.

B. Directions

Write and then diagram two sentences. Show the subject, the linking verb, and the predicate nominative.

SENTENCES—DIAGRAMS

Statement

A *diagram* is a drawing that explains the structure of a sentence.

A. Directions

Diagram the sentences.

Show the noun or pronoun, the linking verb, and the predicate adjective.

subject	linking verb	predicate adjective
(noun)		

1. The horses were fast.

2. Apples are good.

3. That baby is happy.

4. Poplars grow tall.

5. A lemon tastes sour.

6. The quilt is blue.

7. Those workers were tired.

8. The pillow feels soft.

9. The lecture was long.

10. The child seems healthy.

B. Directions

Write and then diagram two sentences. Show the subject, the linking verb, and the predicate adjective.

SENTENCES—DIAGRAMS

Statement

A *diagram* is a drawing that explains the structure of a sentence.

A. Directions

Diagram the sentences.

Show the subject—noun or pronoun; verb—action or linking; complement—direct object, predicate nominative, or predicate adjective; and modifiers—adjectives or adverbs.

1. The industrious student completed the long assignment rapidly.

2. The Irish girl played the golden harp softly.

3. A busy waiter served the flaming dessert flamboyantly.

4. Talented Susan selected the musical program carefully.

5. Small acorns become large trees.

6. The little girls are graceful dancers.

7. Busy Tim was the former president.

8. The race horses were very fast.

9. The gusty wind felt extremely cold.

10. The silver stars sparkled brightly.

B. Directions

Write three sentences that would correspond to the following diagrams:

1. subject | action verb | direct object

2. subject | linking verb \ predicate nominative

3. subject | linking verb \ predicate adjective

SENTENCES—SUBJECT AND PREDICATE   ADJECTIVES AND ADVERBS

Statement

Every sentence has two parts—a *subject* and a *predicate*.

Adjectives modify nouns.

Adverbs modify verbs, adjectives, or other adverbs.

A. Directions

Underline the subject once and the verb twice.

1. The best cook in the class joyfully baked the cakes.

2. A clear brook ripples softly over the rocks.

3. That green gem in the bracelet sparkled brightly.

4. The biggest ship on the lake glided serenely across the water.

5. Little squirrels with bushy tails munched the nuts greedily.

6. The strong athlete trains regularly in the gym.

7. The old car with many dents rattled loudly down Main Street.

8. A gusty wind quickly lifted the kite above the trees.

9. The lonesome man in the blue coat cried sadly.

10. Those frisky puppies across the street played zestfully on the grass.

B. Directions

List the adjectives and adverbs in each of the sentences above.

SENTENCES—DIAGRAMS

Statement

A *diagram* is a drawing that explains the structure of a sentence.

A. Directions

Diagram the sentences.

Adjective prepositional phrases modify nouns.

Adverbial prepositional phrases modify verbs.

EXAMPLE:

The guests at the resort sat happily by the river.

1. The best cook in the class joyfully baked the cakes.

2. A clear brook ripples softly over the rocks.

3. That green gem in the bracelet sparkled brightly.

4. The biggest ship on the lake glided serenely across the water.

5. Little squirrels with bushy tails munched the nuts greedily.

6. The strong athlete trains regularly in the gym.

7. The old car with many dents rattled loudly down Main Street.

8. A gusty wind quickly lifted the kite above the trees.

9. The lonesome man in the blue coat cried sadly.

10. Those frisky puppies across the street played zestfully on the grass.

B. Directions

Write two sentences. Use an adjective prepositional phrase in one and an adverbial prepositional phrase in the other. Diagram the sentences.

SENTENCES—DIAGRAMS

Statement

A *diagram* is a drawing that explains the structure of a sentence.

A. Directions

Diagram the sentences.

Show the noun, verb, direct object, indirect object, and modifiers.

1. Three students brought the teacher red roses.

2. Yolanda will mail Joan the box of books before the fifteenth.

3. The teacher read the children an adventure story.

4. The gentleman offered Aunt Helen his seat on the bus.

5. Cathy showed Roxanna our photo album.

6. Kendall sent Anna pink carnations.

7. The eager salesman quoted Andy the price of the car.

8. That company sent me the cassettes.

9. Blake gave them directions to the airport.

10. An expert guide showed the fisherman the best location.

B. Directions

Write two sentences. Include a noun, verb, direct object, indirect object, and modifiers in each sentence. Diagram the sentences.

SENTENCES—DIAGRAMS

Statement

A *diagram* is a drawing that explains the structure of a sentence.

A. Directions

Diagram the sentences.

Show the noun, verb, direct object, indirect object, and modifiers.

noun		verb		direct object
adj.				adj.
	X	indirect object		

1. Brent gave Jennifer the extra tickets.

2. Billy baked his mom a cherry pie.

3. Meg gave Linda the blue scarf.

4. I read Grandfather the directions for the game.

5. Rosa taught Danny a Chinese song.

6. The driver showed the passengers the interesting sights.

7. Fran sent the baby a rattle.

8. Father bought me a telescope.

9. The seamstress made the dancers new costumes.

10. Mother brought the boys shells from the beach.

B. Directions

Write two sentences. Include a noun, verb, direct object, indirect object, and modifiers in each sentence. Diagram the sentences.

SENTENCES—DIAGRAMS

Statement

A *diagram* is a drawing that explains the structure of a sentence.

A. Directions

Diagram the sentences.

Show the compound subject—two nouns of equal value. They are joined by a coordinate conjunction.

If there are complements in the sentences, show those, too.

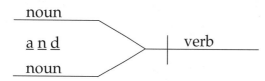

1. Melvin and Grady entered the contest.

2. Della and Carl joined the team.

3. Dave and Ken played tennis.

4. The king and queen attended the ceremony.

5. Elsa and Leo are lions.

6. Jan and Latoya are artists.

7. Will Mike or Todd go to the picnic?

8. Will Kim or Kevin ring the bell?

9. Mark or Susan will meet them at the airport.

10. Poems and stories were read to the class.

B. Directions

Write two sentences. Use compound subjects. Diagram the sentences.

SENTENCES—DIAGRAMS

Statement

A *diagram* is a drawing that explains the structure of a sentence.

A. Directions

Diagram the sentences.

Show the compound verb—two verbs of equal value. They are joined by a coordinate conjunction.

If there are complements in the sentences, show those, too.

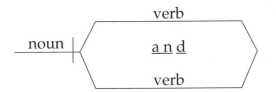

1. Stars twinkle and shine in the sky.

2. The students study and practice daily.

3. He dusted and polished the furniture.

4. Lively children jump and run on the playground.

5. They sang and played in the class recital.

6. The artist sketched and painted the pastoral scene.

7. The boys rowed boats and rode horses at camp.

8. The girls packed and mailed the packages.

9. The children made the sandwiches and poured the milk.

10. They ate dinner and watched television.

B. Directions

Write two sentences. Use compound verbs. Diagram the sentences.

SENTENCES—DIAGRAMS

Statement

A *diagram* is a drawing that explains the structure of a sentence.

A. Directions

Diagram the sentences.

Show the compound direct objects.

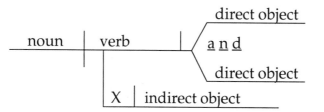

1. Carlos brought her lilacs and roses.

2. Brad peeled potatoes and apples.

3. The teacher read the class stories and poems.

4. Dana played golf and tennis.

5. The mail carrier delivered letters and packages.

6. Jeff packed a sweater and a raincoat.

7. I read *David Copperfield* and *The Pickwick Papers*.

8. The committee served doughnuts and cider.

9. Did he play the violin and the trumpet?

10. She dusted the table and chairs.

B. Directions

Write two sentences. Use compound direct objects. Diagram the sentences.

SENTENCES—DIAGRAMS

Statement

A *diagram* is a drawing that explains the structure of a sentence.

A. Directions

Diagram the sentences.

Show compound indirect objects.

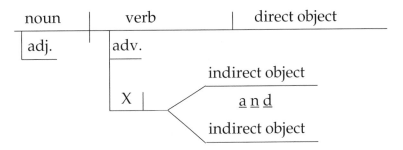

1. They gave Rick and me tickets to the game.

2. Aunt Arlene bought Jen and Mark new sunglasses.

3. Jack wrote Bob and Steve a letter about the reunion.

4. I sent Rosemary and Jason the crate of apples.

5. Meg read Ellen and Tony three stories about pirates.

6. The coach showed Alex and Anna the new equipment.

7. That grocer extended him and me credit.

8. Monica baked Kate and Clark cookies.

9. The salesman sold Dave and Will new raincoats.

10. The principal told the teachers and the students the results of the election.

B. Directions

Write two sentences. Use compound indirect objects. Diagram the sentences.

SENTENCES—DIAGRAMS

Statement

A *diagram* is a drawing that explains the structure of a sentence.

A. Directions

Diagram the sentences.

Show the compound predicate nominatives or compound predicate adjectives.

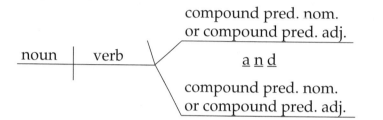

1. The balloons were red and blue.

2. I am hungry and thirsty.

3. The candy was soft and chewy.

4. Tim was a teacher and a coach.

5. *Gone with the Wind* is a book and a movie.

6. Lauren was weary and sleepy.

7. Lincoln was the president and a lawyer.

8. Books are interesting and informative.

9. Leroy is a dancer and a singer.

10. Gene will be the director and the producer.

B. Directions

Write two sentences. Use compound predicate nominatives in one and compound predicate adjectives in the other. Diagram the sentences.

SENTENCES—COMPOUND

Statement

Compound sentences have two or more independent clauses that are usually joined by a coordinate conjunction. The clauses must contain closely connected thoughts.

independent clause   independent clause

c o n j.

A. *Directions*

Determine the independent clauses, circle the conjunctions, and diagram the sentences.

1. Anthony made a cake, but Lynn made a pie.

2. Melba played the piano, and the choir sang songs.

3. Bert erased the chalkboard, and Amanda sharpened the pencils.

4. The slick streets were dangerous, but Warren drove carefully.

5. The children picked the large blackberries, and their mother made a cobbler.

6. Will the committee appoint the captain, or will we elect her?

7. Greg will drive his car, but Mary will ride her horse.

8. The man could not find the street, nor could the merchant give him directions.

9. Donna set the plates on the table, but Alan cooked the dinner.

10. Thomas Alva Edison invented the electric light, and Alexander Graham Bell invented the telephone.

B. *Directions*

Write two sentences. Use two independent clauses joined by a coordinate conjunction in each sentence. Diagram the sentences.

SENTENCES—COMPLEX

Statement

Complex sentences contain an *independent clause* and one or more *dependent clauses*. A dependent clause has an introductory word that connects the clause to the rest of the sentence. The connecting word may be a subordinate conjunction or a relative pronoun.

EXAMPLE: When the bell rang, the students bolted through the front door.

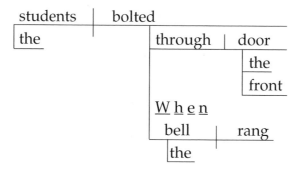

A. Directions

Diagram the sentences.

1. Because the conductor was ill, the concert was canceled.
2. After the ship docked, leis were placed around the necks of the passengers.
3. Unless it rains, we will have the picnic on Sunday.
4. Although she had read the book, she enjoyed the movie.
5. After he uses his plow, the farmer will sow the seeds.
6. I know the woman who made that report.
7. As they were hitched to the troika, the horses stood three abreast.
8. He lost a jacket that fit that description.
9. While they danced, the band played a polka.
10. The painting, which was purchased without a frame, was not included in the exhibit.

B. Directions

Write two complex sentences.

SENTENCES—SIMPLE, COMPOUND, COMPLEX

Statement

A *simple sentence* consists of one independent clause.

A *compound sentence* consists of two or more independent clauses. A *complex sentence* consists of one independent clause and one or more dependent clauses.

A. Directions

On the blanks before the sentences, write *simple*, *compound*, or *complex*.

_____ 1. Captain Nemo steered the *Nautilus*.

_____ 2. Kelly made the cake, and Cody wrapped the gift.

_____ 3. When Bill has a long list, he shops at the supermarket.

_____ 4. The basketball team won every game, but the football team lost five games.

_____ 5. That man, who won the prize, left early.

_____ 6. When you came, I was asleep.

_____ 7. The students read the books by Dickens and Scott.

_____ 8. Her teak tables had been carved in Malaysia.

_____ 9. Chad reserved the auditorium, and Linda notified the members.

_____ 10. As the crew rowed the scull to victory, the crowd cheered wildly.

B. Directions

Write two simple sentences, two compound sentences, and two complex sentences.

SENTENCES—SIMPLE, COMPOUND, COMPLEX

Statement

A *simple sentence* consists of one independent clause.

A *compound sentence* consists of two or more independent clauses. A *complex sentence* consists of one independent clause and one or more dependent clauses.

A. Directions

On the blanks before the sentences, write *simple, compound,* or *complex.* Then diagram the sentences.

_____ 1. Long John Silver was a crafty pirate.

_____ 2. A raccoon washed the food in the cold stream.

_____ 3. As the grasshopper leaped and sang, the ant stored food for winter.

_____ 4. Jane Austen wrote *Emma,* and Mary Wollstonecraft Shelley wrote *Frankenstein.*

_____ 5. The Parthenon is located in Greece, and the Pantheon is located in Italy.

_____ 6. Samuel Johnson and Noah Webster were lexicographers.

_____ 7. Kilimanjaro is the highest point in Africa, and Fujiyama is the highest point in Japan.

_____ 8. Joe worried about the test because he was not prepared.

_____ 9. Milk is liquid, but ice cream is solid.

_____ 10. If you read the story, you can write a good report.

B. Directions

Write a simple sentence, a compound sentence, and a complex sentence. Diagram the sentences.

SENTENCES—SIMPLE, COMPOUND, COMPLEX

Statement

A *simple sentence* consists of one independent clause.

A *compound sentence* consists of two or more independent clauses. A *complex sentence* consists of one independent clause and one or more dependent clauses.

A. Directions

On the blanks before the sentences, write *simple, compound,* or *complex.*

_____ 1. The black dog barked ferociously at the stranger.

_____ 2. Frederic Chopin was a Polish composer, and Claude Debussy was a French composer.

_____ 3. As the mellow sound of music filled the air, the dancers glided around the room.

_____ 4. If she buys her ticket early, she will save money.

_____ 5. A green balloon sailed high in the air.

_____ 6. Henri Matisse was known for bold brush strokes, but Claude Monet was known for feathery brush strokes.

_____ 7. After he fell, he was taken to the hospital.

_____ 8. The aroma of fresh bread drifted from the kitchen.

_____ 9. Benny Goodman was the "King of Swing," and John Philip Sousa was the "March King."

_____ 10. Captain Ahab chased Moby Dick in the *Pequod,* and Richard Henry Dana spent two years at sea in the *Pilgrim.*

B. Directions

Write a simple sentence, a compound sentence, and a complex sentence. Diagram the sentences.

ARTS OF SPEECH

Statement

The way a word is used in a sentence determines the part of speech.

A. Directions

Fill in the blanks.

1. Nouns that name things one can see or touch are _____ nouns; if they name qualities or ideas, they are _____ nouns, and if they name a group of people or things thought of as a unit, they are _____ nouns.

2. The five kinds of pronouns are _____ , _____ , _____ , _____ , and _____ .

3. A helping verb is called an _____ verb.

4. The tenses of a verb are_____ , _____ , _____ , _____ , _____ , and _____ .

5. A list of a verb's forms is called _____ .

6. A word that describes, limits, or points out information is an _____ .

7. The degrees of comparison of adjectives are _____ , _____ , and _____ .

8. Adverbs answer the questions _____ , _____ , _____ , and _____ .

9. Words that join a noun or pronoun to other words in the sentence are called _____ .

10. A _____ conjunction joins words or clauses of equal value.

    A _____ conjunction joins clauses of unequal value.

    _____ conjunctions are used in pairs.

B. Directions

The three principal parts of a verb are present, past, and past participle.
Write the principal parts of the regular verb *call* and the irregular verb *ring*.

⁄NTAX

Statement

Syntax is sentence structure; it is the way in which words are put together to form sentences.

A. Directions

Fill in the blanks.

1. A _____ must have a subject and a predicate and express a complete thought.

2. _____ are drawings that explain the structure of a sentence.

3. A _____ is a group of related words that has no subject or predicate.

4. A clause is a group of words that contains a subject and a predicate.
   An _____ clause stands alone.
   A _____ clause depends on the rest of the sentence.

5. A _____ sentence contains two independent clauses joined by a coordinate conjunction.

6. A _____ sentence contains one independent clause and one or more dependent clauses joined by a subordinate conjunction.

7. _____ are words that are needed to complete the meaning of a sentence.

8. _____ , _____ , _____ , and _____ are complements.

9. Name the action verb and ask *what* or *whom* to find the
_____. The _____ tells *to whom* or *for whom* something was done.

10. _____ and _____ follow linking verbs and refer back to the subject.

B. Directions

Write a sentence that contains a direct object and an indirect object. Write a sentence that contains a predicate adjective.

SENTENCES

Statement

Declarative sentences state facts. *Interrogative* sentences ask questions. *Imperative* sentences make requests or commands. *Exclamatory* sentences express strong feelings.

A. Directions

Write *declarative*, *interrogative*, *imperative*, or *exclamatory* on the blanks before the sentences.

_____ 1. What is Shangri-la?

_____ 2. Everest, Fujiyama, Kilimanjaro, and Matterhorn are mountains.

_____ 3. Alas! The *Hindenburg* burst into flames!

_____ 4. Tales of valuable treasure lured the pirate to the high seas.

_____ 5. In what book do we meet the Cheshire Cat?

_____ 6. Marco Polo met Kublai Khan in China.

_____ 7. Who was the first man to walk on the moon?

_____ 8. Hurray! The last seconds of that game took my breath away!

_____ 9. Return her phone call immediately.

_____ 10. Brutus betrayed Caesar.

B. Directions

1. Answer questions 1, 5, and 7 in complete sentences.
2. Who was Kublai Khan?
3. Locate the mountains:

Everest   _____

Fujiyama   _____

Kilimanjaro   _____

Matterhorn   _____

PUNCTUATION

Statement

Sentences begin with capital letters. The *end punctuation* is determined by the thought expressed. There are four kinds of sentences—*declarative, interrogative, imperative,* and *exclamatory.*

A. Directions

Write *declarative, interrogative, imperative,* or *exclamatory* on the blanks before the sentences. Punctuate the sentences, and capitalize when necessary.

_____ 1. call the fire department

_____ 2. which book contains the most information

_____ 3. did you know there are sixteen ounces in a pint

_____ 4. finish your homework before you leave

_____ 5. pull the plug quickly

_____ 6. the paper was delivered early this morning

_____ 7. halt don't move

_____ 8. zora neale hurston was the author of *their eyes were watching god.*

_____ 9. can you answer that question

_____ 10. place the order before the first of the month

B. Directions

Write four sentences—declarative, interrogative, imperative, and exclamatory. Punctuate each correctly, and use appropriate capitalization.

PUNCTUATION

Statement

Sentences begin with capital letters. The *end punctuation* is determined by the thought expressed. There are four kinds of sentences—*declarative, interrogative, imperative,* and *exclamatory.*

A. Directions

Write *declarative, interrogative, imperative,* or *exclamatory* on the blanks before the sentences.

Punctuate the sentences, and capitalize when necessary.

_____ 1. what was the name of captain nemos seacraft

_____ 2. watch out for the fast train

_____ 3. park the car in front of the house

_____ 4. did you remember to bring the tickets

_____ 5. please list all of the facts

_____ 6. the paper was delivered early this morning

_____ 7. look those planes are going to collide

_____ 8. how tall is alex

_____ 9. the white knight won the joust

_____ 10. walt whitman wrote *leaves of grass*

B. Directions

Fill in the blanks.

1. Use a _____ for the first word in a sentence and for proper nouns.

2. Use an _____ to show possession or a contraction.

3. _____ is the understood subject of an imperative sentence.

PUNCTUATION

Statement

Commas separate word groups and indicate a pause.

A. Directions

Punctuate the following sentences. Use the basic rules for applying commas, end punctuation, and capitalization.

1. gloria will you read the announcement at the nine o'clock meeting

2. he ordered furniture a computer and a painting for his new office

3. why are you so late asked the teacher

4. the zuni a tribe of native americans are known for their weaving pottery and turquoise jewelry

5. holly registered for geometry and henry registered for algebra

6. wilkins micawber sidney carton and uriah heep are interesting characters from stories by charles dickens

7. commander james lawrence said dont give up the ship

8. name the six wives of henry VIII jennifer

9. mary ordered coconut pie but betty chose peach pie

10. who was genghis khan asked charles

B. Directions

Write three sentences, and punctuate them correctly. Use words in a series. Use a direct quotation. Use a nonrestrictive clause.

PUNCTUATION

Statement

Commas separate word groups and indicate a pause.

A. Directions

Punctuate the following sentences. Use the basic rules for applying commas, end punctuation, and capitalization.

1. josephine napoleon's wife was empress of france

2. no I did not order the tickets

3. since he was a famous pianist a large crowd gathered for his recital

4. it is I think the best way to solve that problem

5. the white house is located at 1600 pennsylvania avenue washington d c

6. abraham lincoln delivered the gettysburg address on november 19 1863

7. the liberty bell a symbol of american independence was rung on july 8 1776

8. the limpopo a river in s e africa empties into the indian ocean

9. yes I have finished the report

10. because it is cold in chicago you should pack your gloves and boots

B. Directions

Write three sentences, and punctuate them correctly. Use an appositive. Use a dependent clause. Use an independent element.

PUNCTUATION—COMMAS

Statement

Commas separate word groups and indicate a pause.

A. Directions

Punctuate the following sentences. Use the basic rules for applying commas, end punctuation, and capitalization.

1. watson did you discover any clues

2. she asked when will the plane arrive

3. springfield which is the capital is the site of the illinois state fair

4. sue will I am sure want a ticket

5. no she didn't finish the lesson before noon

6. he celebrated his birthday on march 17 1960 in dallas texas

7. when the whistle blew the factory workers went home

8. mr martin the nurse assisted dr barnes in the operating room

9. we had berries sweet rolls and milk for breakfast

10. she is a kind employer and he is a reliable employee

B. Directions

Write three sentences. Use commas, and tell why each comma was necessary—series, appositive, date, etc.

PUNCTUATION

Statement

Semicolons indicate stronger pauses than commas.

Colons indicate the strongest break.

Apostrophes show possession or ownership. They are also used in contractions.

Quotation marks enclose a person's exact words.

Abbreviations and *initials* are followed by a period.

A. Directions

Punctuate the following sentences. Use the basic rules for applying commas, end punctuation, and capitalization.

1. captain flint was long john silvers parrot

2. ive presented the outline henry will fill in the details

3. the plane will arrive at 417

4. some birds mentioned in classical literature include the following an albatross a raven a roc a skylark and a woodpecker

5. mr and mrs moreno will attend the 800 p m session

6. cleopatra a queen of egypt lived from 69 to 30 b c

7. alex has an appointment with dr marston the dentist

8. i cant read your writing nor can i understand your thinking declared mr keebles

9. peter pans adventures took place in never never land alices adventures happened in wonderland

10. who said give me liberty or give me death inquired the history professor

B. Directions

Write a sentence using a semicolon. Write a sentence using quotation marks.

PUNCTUATION

Statement

Commas separate word groups and indicate a pause.

A. Directions

List the reasons for the commas in these sentences.

_____ 1. Amy, place the order before May 21, 1999.

_____

_____ 2. Columbia is the capital of South Carolina, and Bismarck is the capital of North Dakota.

_____ 3. Adam, a voracious reader, finished seven books this week.

_____ 4. Yes, the graduates wore mortarboards.

_____ 5. The Seine, Rhine, and Volga are rivers.

_____ 6. "Babe was the name of Paul Bunyan's ox," said Glen.

_____ 7. If she fails the test, she can't play in the game on Saturday.

_____ 8. We are too late, I think, to see the whole performance.

_____ 9. That man, who coached the team, is my dad.

_____ 10. The next century will begin on January 1, 2001.

B. Directions

Write three sentences, and punctuate them correctly. Use a proper noun in direct address. Use an appositive. Use words in a series.

CAPITALIZATION

Statement

Capital letters are used in the following situations:

- first word of a sentence and each line of poetry
- proper nouns
- people's titles
- geographical names
- days of the week
- months of the year
- holidays

A. Directions

Punctuate the following sentences. Capitalize when necessary.

1. we celebrate thanksgiving on the fourth thursday in november

2. who was ho chi minh

3. hamlet the prince of denmark wanted to avenge his fathers murder

4. harvard university the oldest university in the united states is located in cambridge massachusetts

5. make an appointment with dr morton for next friday

6. the next tour will include sweden france italy and austria

7. marvin and marlene enrolled in the following classes art geometry history and french

8. mayor valdez notified senator crandall of the monday meeting

9. we celebrate new years eve on december 31.

10. addis ababa is the largest city in ethiopia

Directions

Write a sentence—include holidays and months of the year.
Write a second sentence—include names of places and days of the week.
Punctuate the sentences correctly. Capitalize when necessary.

CAPITALIZATION

Statement
Titles of books and sections of the country are capitalized. Directions (north, south, east, and west) and seasons are not capitalized.

A. Directions
Punctuate the following sentences. Capitalize when necessary.

1. the house of seven gables was written by nathaniel hawthorne

2. robins are harbingers of spring

3. sophomores study english geometry spanish and biology

4. the skiers met in vail colorado last winter

5. the civil war was a conflict between the north and the south

6. fern wilbur and charlotte are characters in e b whites book charlottes web

7. mapleton the new school is three blocks east of main street

8. mexico is south of the united states

9. jesse james wyatt earp and buffalo bill cody were colorful figures of the wild west

10. hamlet prince of denmark is a drama by william shakespeare

B. Directions
Write a sentence about a book using its title, and punctuate it correctly. Write a second sentence about the seasons of the year, and punctuate it correctly. Capitalize when necessary.